Endorsements

"There is nothing better than following Christ, but there is also nothing harder than following Christ. With the care of a shepherd, Dr. John MacArthur takes us back to Scripture and instructs us how to be a Christian all over again. But he does so by invigorating us with a holy joy, a selfless love, and a sturdy humility. He takes us to our knees in prayer, not only to commune with the living God but to equip us with the grace needed to finish the race. Whether you are ready to begin the race or exhausted from running, Dr. MacArthur is ready to run by your side even carry you to the finish line if he must—so that together you hear those words, "Well done, good and faithful servant." If you want to know how to run like a Christian, then let this book be your coach."

—Dr. Matthew Barrett
Associate professor of Christian theology
Midwestern Baptist Theological Seminary, Kansas City, Mo.

"In a society that increasingly looks like the infamous ancient city of Corinth, the church needs vigorous, strong, consistent, powerful Christians (1 Cor. 16:13–14). In this succinct, much-needed, and highly recommended book, Dr. John MacArthur reminds us that true Christian power is not popularity or favor with this world, but the supernatural strength to persevere in uncompromising holiness, sacrificial love, and fervent prayer."

—Dr. Joel R. Beeke
President and professor of systematic theology and homiletics
Puritan Reformed Theological Seminary, Grand Rapids, Mich.

STAND FIRM

STAND FIRM

LIVING IN A POST-CHRISTIAN CULTURE

JOHN MACARTHUR

IR *Reformation Trust*   A DIVISION OF LIGONIER MINISTRIES, ORLANDO, FL

Stand Firm: Living in a Post-Christian Culture
© 2020 by John MacArthur

Published by Reformation Trust Publishing
a division of Ligonier Ministries
421 Ligonier Court, Sanford, FL 32771
Ligonier.org   ReformationTrust.com

Printed in York, Pennsylvania
Maple Press
0000120
First edition

ISBN 978-1-64289-221-5 (Hardcover)
ISBN 978-1-64289-222-2 (ePub)
ISBN 978-1-64289-223-9 (Kindle)

Cover design: Metaleap Creative
Interior design and typeset: Katherine Lloyd, The DESK

Unless otherwise noted, Scripture quotations are taken from the New American Standard Bible® (NASB), Copyright © 1960, 1962, 1963, 1968, 1971, 1972, 1973, 1975, 1977, 1995 by The Lockman Foundation. Used by permission. www.Lockman.org.

Scripture quotations marked ESV are from the ESV® Bible (The Holy Bible, English Standard Version®), copyright © 2001 by Crossway, a publishing ministry of Good News Publishers. Used by permission. All rights reserved.

Scripture quotations marked NKJV are taken from the New King James Version®. Copyright © 1982 by Thomas Nelson. Used by permission. All rights reserved.

Library of Congress Cataloging-in-Publication Data

Names: MacArthur, John, 1939- author.
Title: Stand firm : living in a post-Christian culture / John MacArthur.
Description: First. | Orlando : Reformation Trust Publishing, 2020. |
  Includes bibliographical references and index.
Identifiers: LCCN 2019025529 (print) | LCCN 2019025530 (ebook) |
  ISBN 9781642892215 (hardback) | ISBN 9781642892222 (epub) |
  ISBN 9781642892239 (kindle edition)
Subjects: LCSH: Christian life. | Fortitude. | Christianity and culture.
Classification: LCC BV4509.5 .M2526 2020 (print) | LCC BV4509.5
  (ebook) | DDC 248.4--dc23
LC record available at https://lccn.loc.gov/2019025529
LC ebook record available at https://lccn.loc.gov/2019025530

CONTENTS

Chapter One

THE CHRISTIAN LIFE MEANS BEING CALLED TO HOLINESS

The New Testament resounds with calls to holiness. We are told to abstain from fleshly lusts (1 Peter 2:11), mortify the deeds of the body (Rom. 8:13), love not the world (1 John 2:15), flee immorality (1 Cor. 6:18), put off the old man (Eph. 4:22), and think on what is true (Phil. 4:8). We read commands to let the Word of Christ dwell in us richly (Col. 3:16), to put on the breastplate of righteousness (Eph. 6:14), to buffet our bodies to bring them into subjection (1 Cor. 9:27), and to present our bodies as living sacrifices (Rom. 12:1). We hear the call of the Apostle Paul to cleanse ourselves from all filthiness of the flesh (2 Cor. 7:1), walk in the Spirit (Gal. 5:16), and lay aside all bitterness, anger, and malice (Eph. 4:31). Peter quoted from Leviticus in his charge to live disciplined, godly lives: "Like the Holy One who called you, be holy yourselves also in all your behavior; because it is written, 'You shall be holy, for I am holy'" (1 Peter 1:15–16). Most Christians are well versed in those commands—we know them and we believe them.

However, familiarity and mental assent are not enough to produce righteous results. In fact, the church seems to be rapidly losing the battle for holiness and purity. Consider the worldliness that pervades the church today. Some congregations are virtually indistinguishable from the world; many more are moving fast on a similar trajectory. Others don't necessarily wear their worldly affections on their sleeves, but their outward acts of piety and devotion cannot conceal the corruption within.

The reason is simple. The battle for holiness is not primarily about public professions and external displays. Rather, if God's people are going to be holy, we must first win the battle on the inside.

The Highest Court of the Human Heart

When Paul was forced to defend himself to the believers in Corinth against the accusations of the false apostles, he did not appeal to the testimonies of friends and ministry partners to verify his virtue. He didn't point to his miraculous works or the number of churches he had planted to validate his Apostolic credentials. Instead, he appealed to the highest court of the human heart. "For our proud confidence is this: the testimony of our conscience, that in holiness and godly sincerity, not in fleshly wisdom but in the grace of God, we have conducted ourselves in the world, and especially toward you" (2 Cor. 1:12). Paul called on his own conscience as his best defense.

The value of a clear conscience is a repeated theme throughout Paul's ministry. In Acts 23:1, he said to the Sanhedrin, "Brethren, I have lived my life with a perfectly good conscience before God up to this day." In Acts 24:16, he confessed to Felix, "I also do my best to maintain always a blameless conscience both before God and before men." And in 2 Timothy 1:3, he wrote, "I thank God, whom I serve with a clear conscience."

In his first epistle to Timothy, Paul explained that "the goal of our instruction is love from a pure heart and a good conscience and a sincere faith" (1 Tim. 1:5). He urged his young apprentice in the faith to "fight the good fight, keeping faith and a good conscience" (vv. 18–19). He would later identify "holding to the mystery of the faith with a clear conscience" (3:9) as one of the necessary qualifications for deacons.

Peter likewise understood the value of a clear conscience. In his first epistle, he charged his readers to "keep a good conscience so that in the thing in which you are slandered, those who revile your good behavior in Christ will be put to shame" (1 Peter 3:16). External accusations cannot compare in intensity to the internal testimony of one's own conscience. The Puritan preacher Richard Sibbes described the conscience as "the soul reflecting on itself."[1] In the courtroom of the human heart, the conscience occupies all the roles. It is the *court reporter*, recording in precise detail everything we do (Jer. 17:1). It is our *prosecutor*, lodging complaints when we are guilty, and our *defender* who pleads our innocence (Rom. 2:15). As we see from Paul, the conscience is our *witness*, faithfully testifying for or against us (2 Cor. 1:12). It's our *judge* in both condemnation and vindication (1 John 3:20–21). The conscience even serves as our *executioner*, as it plagues us with grief over our uncovered guilt (1 Sam. 24:5).[2]

The false teachers in Corinth made every attempt to tarnish Paul's testimony and call his credentials into question. But their accusations could not sway or silence the clear testimony of his conscience. In the courtroom of his heart, before the Lord, the Apostle knew he was innocent of their allegations.

When we speak of winning the battle for holiness on the inside, we are speaking of the conscience. Victory in the external battle must be preceded by victory in this internal battle. John Owen wrote, "Let not that man think he makes any progress in holiness who walks not over the bellies of his lusts."[3] True holiness must begin on the inside, and the conscience is the primary contact point for that internal reformation.

That reality flies in the face of the world's view of the conscience. Today we're told to ignore the internal pleading of guilt and grief—to take whatever steps necessary to silence the conscience. One author described guilt as a useless neurosis, saying, "Guilt zones must be exterminated, spray-cleaned and sterilized forever."[4] Psychologists and gurus will happily echo that sentiment, encouraging those plagued by guilt to overrule, suppress, and silence their consciences. The message is clear: guilt is misplaced; shame is someone else's fault. The world will try to convince us that the conscience is nothing more than a

nagging hindrance to living life to the fullest, a harmful imped-
iment to self-esteem and the pursuit of guilt-free pleasure and
satisfaction.

God's people must not adopt that rebellious perspective.
Rather, we need to recognize that the conscience is one of God's
greatest gifts to mankind.

The Soul's Emergency Warning System

In November 1983, an Avianca Airlines jet crashed in Spain.
The flight had departed from Paris and was on approach to
land at Madrid–Barajas Airport. With the landing gear down
and the flaps extended, the Boeing 747 smashed into a series of
hillsides within ten miles of the airport runway, killing 181 of
the 192 people on board.

The investigation determined that the crash was caused
by human error. The flight crew was highly experienced and
they were familiar with their surroundings, having made several
successful trips into Madrid before that evening. In this case,
they believed they had an accurate grasp of the plane's location
and ignored all warnings to the contrary. The cockpit recorder
captured the computerized voice of the Ground Proximity
Warning System repeatedly urging the crew, "Pull up! Pull up!"
Some say the pilot defiantly shouted, "Shut up, gringo!" and
switched off the device in the final moments before impact.

I can think of no more clear and sobering illustration of the
way the conscience is designed to function and the dire consequences of ignoring it. As Paul warned Timothy, those who

fail to heed the warnings of conscience are bound to "[suffer] shipwreck in regard to their faith" (1 Tim. 1:19).

The conscience is an essential device in every human being, and we need to understand the role it plays in holiness. It is the God-given warning mechanism that tells us when we're on a path to spiritual disaster. In that sense, it parallels physical pain.

Have you considered that pain is a good thing? Pain tells us when something is wrong with our bodies. It alerts us to physical issues we might otherwise overlook, helping us determine what's wrong and helping to prevent further damage in the meantime. More than that, pain is a God-given mechanism to keep us from destroying our bodies. This is why leprosy—or Hansen's disease, as it is known today—is such a terrible threat. Long ago it was presumed that leprosy ate away at a person's extremities—that the disease itself destroyed the fingers, toes, feet, and facial features of its victims. But in the 1800s, it was discovered that leprosy does not consume the body. Rather, leprosy destroys one's nerve endings and sense of touch. It robs its victims of the ability to feel pressure or pain, and those afflicted with the disease literally wear off their own extremities, scratching deep gouges into their skin and destroying their eyes, facial features, and bodies because they cannot feel the damage they're doing to themselves. Pain is God's way of protecting us from ourselves. Likewise, the conscience is a warning system placed in the soul to prevent us from destroying ourselves spiritually.

By God's gracious design, everyone has a conscience. Woven into the fabric of humanity, it is the inner voice that senses moral violation. As the Apostle Paul explains, even overt pagans have an innate sense of right and wrong. "For when Gentiles who do not have the Law do instinctively the things of the Law, these, not having the Law, are a law to themselves, in that they show the work of the Law written in their hearts, their conscience bearing witness and their thoughts alternately accusing or else defending them" (Rom. 2:14–15). The conscience works in tandem with our moral convictions to compel us to do what is right and restrain us from what is wrong. It grants the ability to know oneself—to be self-aware, to contemplate, and to comprehend our thoughts, motives, intentions, and feelings. And as it weighs those moral evaluations, it either accuses or excuses our actions. It indicts or exonerates. It gives a sense of well-being, peace, joy, satisfaction, and fulfillment, or it makes one feel ashamed, guilty, fearful, doubting, disturbed, anxious, and depressed.

The ancient Greeks understood the conscience, identifying it as the goddess Nemesis. She was believed to be the very personification of reverence for moral law, calling men and women to lives of virtue. But she also served as the angel of vengeance. In the end, she would overtake people with full retribution for all their reckless transgressions. Nemesis is often depicted flying swiftly in pursuit of terrified sinners, racing with a flashing sword lifted in her hand, ready to strike them dead. That is the conscience. It has a bullying function in one's life, and it can be the most relentless and disturbing enemy of the sinning soul. On the other hand, we could also call the conscience the truest friend and comforter of a holy heart. It is the most accurate tool we possess to measure the state of our souls. Paul wrote in 1 Corinthians 2:11, "For who among men knows the thoughts of a man except the spirit of the man which is in him?"

However, the conscience is not an infallible authority. For all its importance it falls short of being perfect, so we must not confuse it as some kind of internal divine revelation. As one commentator explains it:

> The conscience is not to be equated with the voice of God or even the moral law, rather it is a human faculty which adjudicates upon human action by the light of the highest standard a person perceives.
>
> Seeing that all of human nature has been affected by sin, both a person's perception of the standard of action required and the function of the conscience itself (as a constituent part of human nature) are also affected by sin. For this reason conscience can never be accorded the position of ultimate judge of one's behavior. It is possible that the conscience may excuse one for that which God will not excuse, and conversely it is equally possible that conscience may condemn a person for that which God allows. The final judgment therefore belongs only to God (cf. 1 Cor. 4:2–5). Nevertheless, to reject the voice of conscience is to court spiritual disaster (cf. 1 Tim. 1:19). We cannot reject the voice of conscience with impunity, but we can modify the highest standard to which it relates by gaining for ourselves a greater understanding of the truth.[5]

Think of the conscience as a skylight rather than lamp. It cannot produce light on its own; it merely allows light to shine through into the soul. Specifically, it conforms and aligns to the highest moral standard each soul perceives, and it prompts its owner to live accordingly. It's a mechanism of the human soul, designed to accurately adjudicate your thoughts, motives, and behavior. But just like the altimeter and radar on an airplane, it requires the right information to function properly.

How to Train Your Conscience

Though everyone has a conscience, not all consciences are the same. Like everything else about people, our consciences are fallen and imperfect. Some are weak and burdensome, bound to unnecessary scruples or a legalistic moral law. Some are shallow and immature, prone to taking unnecessary offense. Others are calloused and cauterized from years of abuse and neglect. And it's not just a question of their varying sensitivities—consciences are also bound to a vast array of sinful standards and man-made moral laws. The Catholic's conscience is bound to the pope, the sacraments, and the traditions of the Roman Catholic Church. The Mormon's conscience is likewise tethered to the rituals and ceremonies of his or her faith. The same goes for Hindus, Buddhists, Muslims, atheists, and agnostics—all their consciences are fixed to the highest moral standard they perceive, whether it was adopted from a religious system or concocted on their own.

In some cases, the conscience has become so corrupted and

perverted by worldly influences that people believe they ought to be lying, cheating, and gossiping. They are convinced there's something wrong with them if they're not routinely getting drunk, taking advantage of others, and engaging in all kinds of immorality. Scripture refers to such people as those "whose glory is in their shame" (Phil. 3:19). Through the prophet Isaiah, the Lord proclaimed, "Woe to those who call evil good, and good evil; who substitute darkness for light and light for darkness; who substitute bitter for sweet and sweet for bitter!" (Isa. 5:20).

If your conscience is to function the way God designed it—if it's going to shed the light of truth into your soul and hold fast to a standard of morality—you need to calibrate it to the light of the highest, purest, truest moral law. You need to conform your conscience to the truth of God's Word.

Like any skylight, the usefulness of the conscience is determined by the amount of pure light that passes through it. A properly functioning conscience is fully informed by the truth of Scripture. When David said, "Your word I have treasured in my heart, that I may not sin against You" (Ps. 119:11), he was confessing his desire for a fully informed conscience. Christ prayed for the same thing for His disciples: "Sanctify them in the truth; Your word is truth" (John 17:17). Holiness comes as a result of the Word of God informing the conscience and the conscience informing the person.

And when the conscience is properly calibrated to biblical truth, it sends accurate, trustworthy warnings. When the conscience reflects on the reality of God's truth and cries, "Pull up!

Pull up!" we must listen! So, how do we keep our consciences functioning at maximum capacity? Let's consider some practical steps.

Cleanse Your Conscience

Before the redeeming work of Christ, there's nothing the sinner can do to cleanse his own conscience. Decades of nothing but unrepentant sin might dull its sensitivity and stifle its cries, but the conscience continues to accumulate guilt. It's the silent witness within, always ready to make its detailed case in the soul's courtroom. That's one of the primary reasons why our culture is dominated by alcohol and drug abuse—sinners are desperate for anything that will silence the cries of a conscience burdened by a lifetime of sin.

It's also why the world's religions of works-righteousness cannot calm or quiet the grief-stricken soul. There is no amount of outward piety that can numb or nullify a lifetime of accumulated guilt. In his heart of hearts, the outwardly pious sinner still knows he's a sinner and that none of his external acts of devotion and supplication can truly satisfy the shouts of his grieved conscience.

The only means for truly cleansing the sinner's conscience is the justifying work of Jesus Christ. Only through belief in the gospel can anyone know freedom from the grief and guilt of our sin. Contrasting the efficacy of Christ's work on the cross with Israel's sacrificial system in the Old Testament, the writer of Hebrews asks, "For if the blood of goats and bulls and the ashes of a heifer sprinkling those who have been defiled sanctify for the cleansing of the flesh, how much more will the blood of Christ, who through the eternal Spirit offered Himself without blemish to God, cleanse your conscience from dead works to serve the living God?" (9:13–14). Only Christ's atoning work can fully satisfy our need for righteousness. Paul describes that glorious reality with these powerful words: "He made Him who knew no sin to be sin on our behalf, so that we might become the righteousness of God in Him" (2 Cor. 5:21). Only through repentance and faith in the sacrifice of Christ can we be made clean.

In faith, we acknowledge the guilt of our sin and trust in the substitutionary death of Christ to pay our eternal debt and secure forgiveness on our behalf. In Him, we have been bought at a price (1 Cor. 6:20), purified (Heb. 1:3), and set aside for good works (Eph. 2:10). Having been made new creations in Christ, our faith informs our conscience that our past sins have been paid for—that we have been washed and pardoned by the work of Christ. In fact, the writer of Hebrews explains that a cleansed conscience goes hand in hand with the assurance of our salvation: "Let us draw near with a sincere heart in full assurance of faith, having our hearts sprinkled clean from an evil conscience and our bodies washed with pure water" (10:22). A cleansed and quiet conscience is sweet comfort to the newly redeemed sinner. And it's not just a one-time cleansing—1 John 1:9 promises, "If we confess our sins, He is faithful and righteous to forgive us our sins and to cleanse us from all unrighteousness." Once the conscience has been cleansed by Christ, it is the believer's job to keep it clear.

Clear Your Conscience

It's the duty of every believer to protect the purity of his conscience—to guard against the presence of unchecked sin and keep short accounts through self-examination and faithful confession. The newly cleansed conscience will be all the more sensitive to sin, so it's important to heed its warnings and keep it clear. That's accomplished on several fronts.

First, we must confess our sins. First John 1:9 says, "If we confess our sins, He is faithful and righteous to forgive us our sins and to cleanse us from all unrighteousness." This should be the pattern of the believer's life—an established routine from which we do not deviate. Proverbs 28:13 gives us additional encouragement to that end: "He who conceals his transgressions will not prosper, but he who confesses and forsakes them will find compassion." David further illustrates the destructive effects of unaddressed sin: "When I kept silent about my sin, my body wasted away through my groaning all day long. For day and night Your hand was heavy upon me; my vitality was drained away as with the fever heat of summer" (Ps. 32:3–4). Instead, we need to long for the freedom and blessing of keeping a clear conscience before the Lord: "I acknowledged my sin to You, and my iniquity I did not hide; I said, 'I will confess my transgressions to the LORD'; and You forgave the guilt of my sin" (v. 5).

In addition to confessing our sins to the Lord, we need to seek forgiveness and reconciliation from anyone else we have sinned against. In the Sermon on the Mount, Christ illustrated the importance of not allowing personal wrongs and grudges to accumulate: "Therefore if you are presenting your offering at the altar, and there remember that your brother has something against you, leave your offering there before the altar and go; first be reconciled to your brother, and then come and present your offering" (Matt. 5:23–24). As children of God, we must likewise cultivate a humble attitude of forgiving others who sin against us. "For if you forgive others for their transgressions, your heavenly Father will also forgive you. But if you do not forgive others, then your Father will not forgive your transgressions" (Matt. 6:14–15). Forgiveness and restoration should be woven into the culture of the church, marking the people of God as distinct from the world.

Along with seeking forgiveness and reconciliation, we need to make restitution to those we've wronged. The Lord included a provision in His law detailing how the Israelites were to pay back their debts to those they sinned against. God said to Moses, "Speak to the sons of Israel, 'When a man or woman commits any of the sins of mankind, acting unfaithfully against the LORD, and that person is guilty, then he shall confess his sins which he has committed, and he shall make restitution in full for his wrong and add to it one-fifth of it, and give it to him whom he has wronged' " (Num. 5:6–7). A lingering debt can cause just as much grief and guilt as active sin. In those cases, true reconciliation isn't possible without restitution.

Finally, keeping a clear conscience means not overlooking its indictments. We need to echo the words of Paul and do our best "to maintain always a blameless conscience both before God and before men" (Acts 24:16). Don't put off addressing your guilt and sin—don't assume it will go away on its own over time. We cannot procrastinate when it comes to dealing with sin. Postponing it inevitably leads to anxiety, depression, and more sin. Allowing sin to linger is an invitation to spiritual cancer. Keeping your conscience clear means addressing guilt and sin immediately, thoroughly, and biblically as soon as you are aware of it.

Strengthen Your Conscience

The smoke detectors in your home are designed to alert you to the presence of a specific, imminent threat. In the same way, the warning lights in the dashboard of your car are intended to make you aware of a malfunction before the damage becomes catastrophic. But what good is an alarm that routinely misfires, constantly alerting you to nonexistent danger? An inaccurate, inconsistent warning system can be as bad as not having a warning system at all—*worse* if you develop a habit of ignoring it altogether.

In the same way, a misfiring, overactive conscience can do more harm than good.

For example, a conscience that is too closely fixed to personal feelings is often untrustworthy. When it rises and falls with inconsistent emotions, the conscience can falsely magnify doubts and fears rather than reflecting the true state of the heart and its affections. The conscience can also be confused by too much focus on failures with sin at the expense of recognizing the work of God's grace. Such imbalance cripples the conscience's ability to accurately weigh spiritual fruit and often leads to unproductive and unhealthy doubts about one's standing with the Lord. To function properly, the conscience must be disconnected from the unpredictable whims of the human heart. If it is to be a reliable guide and guard, it must be informed by God's Word alone.

Another common way to corrupt the conscience is to cultivate an unbiblical emphasis on good works. Many Christians—and particularly new believers—fall into the trap of thinking too much about their personal piety. While they're not necessarily trying to *earn* God's favor, they seem to think it's their job to *secure* and *maintain* it through their efforts and acts of self-discipline. That undue emphasis on externals foolishly alters the focus of the conscience, pointing it outward and shifting its attention away from its intended target, the heart. We must not confuse our consciences with a false notion of righteousness. The most accurate, trustworthy conscience is the one that holds fast to God's Word and eschews all man-made standards.

The most familiar cause for malfunction is what Scripture calls a "weak" conscience (Rom. 14:1). The weak conscience is immature and fragile. It's too quick to accuse and too easily offended. It's prone to fret over matters that wouldn't provoke the conscience of a stronger, more mature believer. In fact, it won't allow the believer to do things he is free to do—the weak conscience puts unbiblical limits on the believer's liberty in Christ. Unlike the seared conscience, which has been dulled to the point of insensitivity, the weak conscience is *hypersensitive*.

Paul devoted significant attention in his epistles to instructing the church in how to care for believers with weak consciences. Those who suffer from a weak conscience most often feel the pangs of guilt over activities and associations that call to mind aspects of their former sinful lives. In the first-century church, the primary issue was whether to eat food that had been offered to idols.

> Therefore concerning the eating of things sacrificed to idols, we know that there is no such thing as an idol in the world, and that there is no God but one. For even if there are so-called gods whether in heaven or on earth, as indeed there are many gods and many lords, yet for us there is but one God, the Father, from whom are all things and we exist for Him; and one Lord, Jesus Christ, by whom are all things, and we exist through Him. However not all men have this knowledge; but some, being accustomed to the idol until now, eat food as if it were sacrificed to an idol; and *their conscience being weak is defiled.* (1 Cor. 8:4–7, emphasis added)

Many of the men and women in the New Testament church had been saved out of paganism and idolatry. While they would have affirmed their faith in the one true God, it likely would have taken some time to fully cast off the familiar influences of their former religious experiences. It's understandable that those immature believers would reject and repudiate their former lives, shunning any aspect of public life that could potentially draw them back into pagan rituals and idol worship. That included eating foods that had previously been offered as a sacrifice to those false gods. Paul was saying that a mature believer could eat without troubling his conscience—that such a believer would know that the food itself had no bearing on his standing before the Lord. He wrote, "But food will not commend us to God; we are neither the worse if we do not eat, nor the better if we do eat" (v. 8). There was nothing inherently spiritual about the food, but it nonetheless posed a problem for those whose consciences were still stinging from their formerly pagan lifestyles. Paul instructed the rest of the church to defer their freedoms for the sake of these weaker brothers.

We could use more of that attitude in the church today, when too many people thoughtlessly exercise and even parade their Christian liberty. They don't give enough thought to the example of their lives and the impact it can have with weaker, less mature brothers and sisters in the faith. Paul's primary concern with the Corinthian church was not eliminating hindrances to the full exercise of their freedom in Christ. Rather, he was urging them to make sure their freedom did not come at a spiritual cost to a fellow believer.

> But take care that this liberty of yours does not some-how become a stumbling block to the weak. For if someone sees you, who have knowledge, dining in an idol's temple, will not his conscience, if he is weak, be strengthened to eat things sacrificed to idols? For through your knowledge he who is weak is ruined, the brother for whose sake Christ died. And so, by sinning against the brethren and wounding their conscience

when it is weak, you sin against Christ. Therefore, if food causes my brother to stumble, I will never eat meat again, so that I will not cause my brother to stumble. (vv. 9–13)

Paul is instructing us to defer the exercise of our liberty in Christ, or even surrender it altogether, for the sake of those who are less mature—those who might fall back into old patterns of sin by following our example. At the same time, he's warning us not to teach weak believers to ignore their consciences, lest it become a habit. We need to be willing to patiently teach and lead young believers in the truth, rather than pushing them to exercise their freedoms too early and violate their consciences.

In a parallel passage in Romans, Paul further exhorts mature believers not to look down on those weaker brothers: "Now accept the one who is weak in faith, but not for the purpose of passing judgment on his opinions" (14:1). But it's not just mature believers who might be tempted to pass judgment: "One person has faith that he may eat all things, but he who is weak eats vegetables only. The one who eats is not to regard with contempt the one who does not eat, and *the one who does not eat is not to judge the one who eats*, for God has accepted him" (vv. 2–3, emphasis added). Here Paul highlights one of the dangers of a weak conscience—that its oversensitivity can be easily mistaken for fastidious spiritual maturity. Some will point to a conscience that is particularly tender and sensitive as a spiritual strength. It's actually the opposite—a liability that often leads to unnecessary offense, an unduly critical spirit, and slow spiritual growth.

Those who nurture a weak conscience are also more susceptible to legalism and self-righteousness, mistaking their list of dos and don'ts as a measure of spiritual maturity.

Throughout Paul's descriptions of the weak conscience, he consistently diagnoses it as a case of spiritual immaturity. He writes that these weaker brothers lack knowledge (1 Cor. 8:7) or are "weak in faith" (Rom. 14:1). The Apostle instructs us to support and defer to these immature believers for a while, but we're not supposed to coddle them permanently. The implication of these passages is that those with weak consciences will—or at least *should*—eventually grow out of that state and progress to further spiritual maturity.

Therefore, strengthening the conscience is a function of growing in love for God and the knowledge of His truth. As the believer's understanding of spiritual truth deepens and he develops godly affections, the attraction of the former, sinful life fades. Those things that once tempted and seduced the heart no longer hold the same allure. And as the world loses its influence, the conscience is less prone to false alarms and unnecessary offense. As believers grow spiritually—that is, as their minds are enlightened by the Word of God and the work of the Holy Spirit, and as their faith is built up in love for Christ and His church—the weak conscience will grow stronger and they will embrace freedom in Christ.

Guard Your Conscience

What good is a state-of-the-art alarm system if you don't pay attention to its flashing lights and wailing sirens? You wouldn't blithely ignore an alert that your house was on fire or that someone was breaking into your car.

In the same way, the believer cannot afford to ignore the cries of the conscience. When it calls us to attention, we need to act. We need to take seriously the warnings it provides and deal swiftly with the sin it identifies. There is no room for a lackadaisical response—we must instantly go to battle with the flesh, thoroughly "putting to death the deeds of the body" (Rom. 8:13). On the other hand, there is no better way to damage and darken the conscience than to let sin reside within us and fester. That is particularly true when it comes to sins of the mind.

Nothing is more destructive and deadly to the conscience than the secret sins of the mind. Indulging in the private thoughts of a wicked imagination is a direct attack on the conscience. It's an act of open defiance, engaging all of one's inner faculties in the vile, vicious assault. Those who nurture sinful thoughts can't hope to have a pure conscience. Sowing such impurity internally corrupts and perverts the conscience, defiling it and rendering it effectively useless over time.

God's people must not buy in to the demonic lie that God is only concerned with the exterior—that sins of the heart and mind are acceptable as long as they remain secret. That false notion undergirded Israel's system of works-righteousness, and it was one of the first things Christ confronted in His public ministry. He declared:

> You have heard that the ancients were told, "You shall not commit murder" and "Whoever commits murder

shall be liable to the court." But I say to you that every-one who is angry with his brother shall be guilty before the court; and whoever says to his brother, "You good-for-nothing," shall be guilty before the supreme court; and whoever says, "You fool," shall be guilty enough to go into the fiery hell. . . . You have heard that it was said, "You shall not commit adultery"; but I say to you that everyone who looks at a woman with lust for her has already committed adultery with her in his heart. (Matt. 5:21–22, 27–28)

In truth, there is no such thing as a private, secret sin. The wicked imagination is merely the seedbed of external sin. No one "falls into" immorality or adultery—the sinner indulged those lustful desires internally long before he ever acted on them. In the same way, the thief's heart was corrupted by covetousness long before he ever stole anything. Wickedly toying with sin internally is the best way to guarantee that it will eventually manifest itself externally. And in the meantime, the conscience is battered and defiled while its cries fall on deaf ears.

We cannot afford the occasional dalliance with sins of the mind. We cannot indulge our sinful imaginations with impunity. If we think the sins of our imagination are truly secret, we're lying to ourselves. There is no corner of our hearts or minds that is hidden from the Lord. David declared: "You understand my thought from afar. You scrutinize my path and my lying down, and are intimately acquainted with all my ways. Even before there is a word on my tongue, behold, O LORD,

You know it all" (Ps. 139:2–4). We need to echo the conviction of Psalm 44:21: "Would not God find this out? For He knows the secrets of the heart." Nothing is secret from the Lord.

God's people also need to remember that our thoughts are the truest test of our character: "For as he thinks within himself, so he is" (Prov. 23:7). What goes on in the deepest recesses of our hearts is the best measure of who we really are. "As in water face reflects face, so the heart of man reflects man" (Prov. 27:19). We need to heed the call of Proverbs 4:23: "Watch over your heart with all diligence, for from it flow the springs of life."

We began by saying the battle for personal holiness is won in the conscience. It's just as easily lost there too. If we're going to have a conscience worth listening to, we must not misinform it, or abuse and defile it. We need to guard it faithfully—most of the time from ourselves.

Charles Wesley wrote more than six thousand hymns; we sing many of them to this day. But one of his best—and sadly, one that I have never heard in a church service—is his personal plea for a tender, godly conscience.

> I want a principle within
> Of watchful, godly fear,
> A sensibility of sin,
> A pain to feel it near.
> Help me the first approach to feel
> Of pride or wrong desire;
> To catch the wandering of my will,
> And quench the kindling fire.

From Thee that I no more may stray,
No more Thy goodness grieve,
Grant me the filial awe, I pray,
The tender conscience give.
Quick as the apple of an eye,
O God, my conscience make!
Awake my soul when sin is nigh,
And keep it still awake.[6]

May that be the prayer of my heart as well.

- Chapter Two -

THE CHRISTIAN LIFE MEANS LOVING YOUR NEIGHBOR AND YOUR ENEMY

F irst-century Jews eagerly anticipated a Messiah who would overthrow the oppressive regime that held them under its abusive, pagan rule. In that regard, they weren't wrong—Christ did come to break the chains that bound Israel. They simply had the wrong regime in mind. Instead of casting off Rome's political and military authority, Christ attacked Israel's apostate religion and its self-righteous rulers.

In the Sermon on the Mount, Jesus delivered a devastating assault on Israel's apostasy. Their religion, made up of human tradition mingled with Old Testament truth, was not at all representative of the purity and authority of God's revealed Word. The Jews had managed to distort every precept of God, lowering His standards to accommodate their sanctimonious self-righteousness. Christ's Sermon on the Mount repeatedly showed how true kingdom living far exceeded the form of apostate Jewish religion that existed at that time. In the course of a few hours, He comprehensively exposed their corruption.

For example, Jesus revealed how the command "You shall not murder" (Ex. 20:13) had been diminished in the hands of Israel's religious leaders. He said, "You have heard that the ancients were told, 'You shall not commit murder' and 'Whoever commits murder shall be liable to the court.' But I say to you that everyone who is angry with his brother shall be guilty before the court; and whoever says to his brother, 'You good-for-nothing,' shall be guilty before the supreme court; and whoever says, 'You fool,' shall be guilty enough to go into the fiery hell" (Matt. 5:21–22). In the same way, He condemned their shallow understanding of the seventh commandment, "You shall not commit adultery" (Ex. 20:14), showing that it extends to the very thoughts and intents of the heart: "You have heard that it was said, 'You shall not commit adultery'; but I say to you that everyone who looks at a woman with lust for her has already committed adultery with her in his heart" (Matt. 5:27–28). He likewise rebuked their wicked tampering with the injunction "You shall not take the name of the LORD your God in vain" (Ex. 20:7), affirming instead that all unnecessary oaths were prohibited (Matt. 5:33–37). And He showed how they had corrupted the principle of "eye for eye, tooth for tooth" (Ex. 21:24), instead exhorting them, "But I say to you, do not resist an evil person; but whoever slaps you on your right cheek, turn the other to him also. If anyone wants to sue you and take your shirt, let him have your coat also" (Matt. 5:39–40).

Finally, He dealt with the vile corruption of the instructions to "love your neighbor as yourself." That would have been a familiar commandment to His listeners, as it was spelled out explicitly in Leviticus 19:17–18: "You shall not hate your fellow countryman in your heart; you may surely reprove your neighbor, but shall not incur sin because of him. You shall not take vengeance, nor bear any grudge against the sons of your people, but you shall love your neighbor as yourself." Jesus addressed their twisted perspective on "loving your neighbor" and, in doing so, provided for us an informative and helpful look at this all-important feature of love. The Lord said:

> You have heard that it was said, "You shall love your neighbor and hate your enemy." But I say to you, love your enemies and pray for those who persecute you, so that you may be sons of your Father who is in heaven; for He causes His sun to rise on the evil and the good, and sends rain on the righteous and the unrighteous. For if you love those who love you, what reward do you have? Do not even the tax collectors do the same? If you greet only your brothers, what more are you doing than others? Do not even the Gentiles do the same? Therefore you are to be perfect, as your heavenly Father is perfect. (Matt. 5:43–48)

As we know, the *second* great commandment—after "Love the Lord your God with all your heart, and with all your soul, and with all your mind" (Matt. 22:37)—is "Love your neighbor as yourself" (v. 39). In fact, the Ten Commandments can be divided into two sections: one section having to do with love toward God, and the other having to do with love toward our neighbor. Essentially, those two key commandments sum up all of God's law. Jesus made that very point, saying, "On these two commandments depend the whole Law and the Prophets" (v. 40).

The Apostle Paul echoed the idea that this simple directive gathers up everything else we've been commanded regarding how we relate to one another: "He who loves his neighbor has fulfilled the law. For this, 'You shall not commit adultery, you shall not murder, you shall not steal, you shall not covet,' and if there is any other commandment, it is summed up in this saying, 'You shall love your neighbor as yourself' " (Rom. 13:8–9). Given Scripture's abundant exhortations on the matter, to understand the importance of loving our neighbor is to recognize the high priority God placed on how we conduct our relationships.

And in the Sermon on the Mount, the Lord Himself speaks to the very heart of this commandment. He pushes past the corrupt traditions and the Scripture twisting of Israel's religious elite, digging down to the foundational truth about how God expects His people to interact with both their neighbors and their enemies.

Leaning on Tradition, Losing the Truth

Throughout Matthew 5, Christ repeatedly employs a phrase to introduce a new point of discussion. Over and over, Jesus uses some variation of His words in Matthew 5:43, "You have heard that it was said." This brief introduction was used to identify the prevailing tradition that dominated Judaism at the time. It was a familiar phrase, used in rabbinical teaching to introduce doctrine and tradition that had been passed down through Israel's history. However, in the mouth of the Lord, it was a subtle way to differentiate Israel's low, defective theology from the truth of Scripture and the clear teaching of God's law. He was effectively alerting His audience that the following statement did not represent God or the Old Testament—it simply reflected the Jews' traditional dogma.

In this case, the rabbinical teaching was a poor and misleading paraphrase of God's commandment in Leviticus 19:17–18. He said, "You have heard that it was said, 'You shall love your neighbor and hate your enemy' " (Matt. 5:43). Comparing this to the words of Leviticus, it's clear that the rabbis had made some alterations. To begin with, they left off the final two words of the original command ("as yourself"), a convenient omission.

It's possible—perhaps even *likely*—that the rabbis and scribes were simply too proud to tolerate the implications of loving anyone else as much as they loved themselves. Remember, these were the same hypocrites Jesus was about to single out for their arrogance and their love for the praise of men. "So when you give to the poor, do not sound a trumpet before you, as the hypocrites do in the synagogues and in the streets, so that they may be honored by men. Truly I say to you, they have their reward in full. . . . When you pray, you are not to be like the hypocrites; for they love to stand and pray in the synagogues and on the street corners so that they may be seen by men" (Matt. 6:2, 5). Even their acts of piety and devotion were staged to draw maximum attention back onto themselves. And although the command to love others the way they loved themselves was unmistakably part of God's law, the prospect of obeying it would have been offensive in the extreme. Such equal love for others would have been an affront to their high view of their own spiritual status. For Israel's religious elite, loving those they considered beneath them as though they were equals would have been inconceivable.

The fact is that it isn't easy for any of us to love someone else as thoroughly as we love ourselves. Our love for ourselves is unfeigned, fervent, habitual, and permanent. It generally respects and prioritizes all our needs, wants, desires, hopes, and ambitions. It consistently promotes our well-being. It does everything possible to secure our own happiness and satisfaction, protect our own welfare, produce our own comfort, and meet all our own interests. It seeks our own pleasure and fulfillment, and it knows no limit of effort to secure all of these things. Scripture says that is exactly how we are to love our neighbor. But Israel's religious elite left that out, reducing "love your neighbor" to something less than such consummate devotion.

Worse still, the rabbis and scribes had narrowed the definition of "neighbor" to exclude virtually everyone but themselves. That meant the command didn't apply to social pariahs like the tax gatherers, who had betrayed their fellow Jews by siding with Rome and extorting their countrymen through excessive taxation. In the eyes of the Pharisees, even sharing a meal with such villains was enough to call your character into question (Matt. 9:11). In the same way, the Jews believed that the command to love one's neighbor did not apply to adulterers, criminals, and other overt sinners (cf. Luke 18:11). Naturally, it excluded all gentiles. In fact, the narrow definition of "neighbor" even left out many of the common folk throughout Israel—for the most part, the religious leaders had nothing but disdain for their fellow Jews. Such exclusivity only served to further feed their prideful, evil hearts.

But it wasn't enough to redact God's instructions and deny vast swaths of the population "neighbor" status—the rabbinical tradition had also *added* a clause to the command. Christ's quote of their teaching indicates that they tacked on a spurious phrase: "You shall love your neighbor *and hate your enemy*" (Matt. 5:43, emphasis added). The law of Leviticus did not have any such limitations. It said nothing about who was considered a neighbor. It didn't separate gentiles or sort out people of a lower socioeconomic status. The divisions the rabbis and scribes were creating and enforcing had no biblical basis whatsoever. In other words, they legitimized antipathy, enmity, and hatred for others by shoehorning it into their theological tradition. Worse, they equated their sinful, self-serving addition with God's Word.

In fact, their teaching overtly contradicted God's law. Leviticus 19:34 says, "The stranger who resides with you shall be to you as the native among you, and you shall love him as yourself." Furthermore, Exodus 12:49 says, "The same law shall apply to the native as to the stranger who sojourns among you." God's law did not change from person to person. It was not limited by ethnic or geographical lines. It set a fixed standard that applied equally to both the Jews and the gentiles in their midst. But the religious elite had conveniently ignored that too.

In order to understand just how deeply this was entrenched, one needs to look at the literature of the time. If you read any of the Essene literature—the Qumran community where the Dead Sea Scrolls were found—you find statements like "Love all that [God] has chosen and hate all that He has rejected."[1] We also find the exhortation to "love all the sons of light, each according to his lot in God's design, and hate all the sons of darkness."[2] For such an exclusive religious sect, that could mean all non-Essenes—that's how isolationist they had become. Across the scope of first-century Judaism, the idea of loving your neighbor had really become a license to hate. One of the maxims of the Pharisees in those days was, "If a Jew sees a gentile fallen into the sea, let him by no means lift him out, for it is written, 'You shall not rise up against the blood of your neighbor,' but this man is not your neighbor." Through their reckless reinterpretation of God's law, they could make a case for allowing a gentile to drown. They had effectively canonized their haughtiness and hatred. That was the dominant religious tradition that Jesus confronted.

Excusing Animosity

One could argue that Israel's relationship to the neighboring nations had been adversarial from the start, that their animosity was divinely decreed. When the Jews first entered the land of Canaan, they were commanded to exterminate the Canaanites:

> When the LORD your God brings you into the land where you are entering to possess it, and clears away many nations before you, the Hittites and the Girgashites and the Amorites and the Canaanites and the Perizzites and the Hivites and the Jebusites, seven nations greater and stronger than you, and when the LORD your God delivers them before you and you defeat them, then you shall utterly destroy them. You shall make no covenant with them and show no favor to them. (Deut. 7:1–2)

Centuries later, did those instructions legitimize the seething animosity Israel held for its neighboring nations in the time of Christ? Did God originally institute the hatred they harbored for the gentiles? And if so, is there a conflict between Christ's words in the Sermon on the Mount and God's instructions in the Old Testament? Dietrich Bonhoeffer shed some helpful light on this seeming contradiction. He wrote: "The wars of Israel were the only 'holy wars' in history, for they were the wars of God against the world of idols. It is not this enmity which Jesus condemns, for then He would have condemned the whole history of God's dealing with His people. On the contrary, He affirms the Old Covenant."[3]

The Lord's commandments to wipe out the idolatrous inhabitants of Canaan weren't the instructions of some bloodthirsty deity. God instructed Israel to destroy those idolatrous nations for the express purpose of preserving the purity of His covenant people.

> Furthermore, you shall not intermarry with them; you shall not give your daughters to their sons, nor shall you take their daughters for your sons. For they will turn your sons away from following Me to serve other gods; then the anger of the LORD will be kindled against you and He will quickly destroy you. But thus you shall do to them: you shall tear down their altars, and smash their sacred pillars, and hew down their Asherim, and burn their graven images with fire. For you are a holy people to the LORD your God; the LORD your God has chosen you to be a people for His own possession out of all the peoples who are on the face of the earth. (vv. 3–6)

God commanded His people to drive out and destroy those wicked nations in order to defend Israel from their idolatrous influence. This was no mere feud—God was purging the land of corrupting influences. He was protecting His people, not establishing a permanent pattern for personal, ethnocentric animosity.

Moreover, the Old Testament law included specific provisions for how the Israelites were to engage with others—even with their enemies. "If you meet your enemy's ox or his donkey wandering away, you shall surely return it to him. If you see the donkey of one who hates you lying helpless under its load, you shall refrain from leaving it to him, you shall surely release it with him" (Ex. 23:4–5). In addition, Proverbs 25:21–22 says, "If your enemy is hungry, give him food to eat; and if he is thirsty, give him water to drink; for you will heap burning coals on his head, and the LORD will reward you." Job summed up how God's people were to view their enemies: "Have I rejoiced at the extinction of my enemy, or exulted when evil befell him? No, I have not allowed my mouth to sin by asking for his life in a curse" (Job 31:29–30).

So, while the Old Testament does include holy wars and pronounces judgment on nations that are the permanent, unrepentant enemies of God, there is no room for personal rancor, vengeance, or hostility. Put simply, the scribes and rabbis could not point back in Israel's history to legitimize or excuse their hatred for the gentiles.

Nor could they point to the imprecatory psalms and the severe curses passed down on people outside of God's covenant. The Psalms contain some scathing rebukes and vicious condemnations for those who oppose the Lord. For example:

May their table before them become a snare;
And when they are in peace, may it become a trap.
May their eyes grow dim so that they cannot see,
And make their loins shake continually.
Pour out Your indignation on them,
And may Your burning anger overtake them.
May their camp be desolate;
May none dwell in their tents.

For they have persecuted him whom You Yourself
   have smitten,
And they tell of the pain of those whom You have
   wounded.
Add iniquity to their iniquity,
And may they not come into Your righteousness.
May they be blotted out of the book of life
And may they not be recorded with the righteous.
(Ps. 69:22–28)

However, this is not an expression of mere personal animosity. David explained earlier in that same psalm, "Zeal for Your house has consumed me, and the reproaches of those who reproach You have fallen on me" (v. 9). It's the same kind of godly, righteous anger he expressed in Psalm 139:21–22: "Do I not hate those who hate You, O Lord? And do I not loathe those who rise up against You? I hate them with the utmost hatred; they have become my enemies." He was not venting his own anger; he was taking up the cause of God against the idolatrous nations that had risen up against His people. He regarded the wicked as enemies of God and the covenant people. The conflicts in view here for David were national, not personal.

It is at that point precisely that the scribes and rabbis never made a distinction. They never distinguished between what was divinely judicial and what was personal. They took the prerogatives that belonged to God in the unfolding of His covenant purpose and they personalized them into their own private relationships. Thus, they perverted God's law of love for neighbors and inhibited the possibility of evangelistic outreach to the idolatrous nations. To love their neighbors would be to ardently desire that they would repent, believe, and enter into a right relationship with God. To hate them would be to desire, with equal ardor, that they would perish in hell. That was the attitude of the Jews in Christ's time, as it had been for centuries.

The prophet Jonah is a prime example of this stance. God called Jonah to preach to Nineveh, the capital city of Assyria, and Jonah fled in the opposite direction. The Assyrians were notorious for their bloodthirsty violence and particularly for the cruelty they showed to Israel. Jonah wanted nothing good for them, and he had no intention of leading them to repentance and faith. And when the people of Nineveh dramatically repented and turned to God, Jonah responded with a fit of rage and frustration:

> But it greatly displeased Jonah and he became angry. He prayed to the LORD and said, "Please LORD, was not this what I said while I was still in my own country? Therefore in order to forestall this I fled to Tarshish, for I knew that You are a gracious and compassionate God, slow to anger and abundant in lovingkindness, and one who relents concerning calamity. Therefore now, O LORD, please take my life from me, for death is better to me than life." (Jonah 4:1–3)

Jonah didn't praise God for the miraculous repentance of the Ninevites. Instead, he begged the Lord to *take his life* so he wouldn't have to witness his enemies entering into a right relationship with God. That's how deeply the Jews hated those they considered their enemies—death itself was preferable to seeing them rescued from hell by divine grace and forgiveness.

Love Your Enemies

In the face of that self-righteous hatred, Christ confrontingly said:

> "But I say to you, love your enemies and pray for those who persecute you, so that you may be sons of your Father who is in heaven; for He causes His sun to rise on the evil and the good, and sends rain on the righteous and the unrighteous. For if you love those who love you, what reward do you have? Do not even the tax collectors do the same? If you greet only your brothers, what more are you doing than others? Do not even the Gentiles do the same? Therefore you are to be perfect, as your heavenly Father is perfect." (Matt. 5:44–48)

This is not just a rebuke and corrective to the rabbinical tradition. This is essentially the Son's commentary on the Old Testament law, unpacking the fullness of what it means to love your neighbor as yourself. We can boil down Christ's teaching here into three simple directives, the first of which is to love your enemies.

Jesus begins by saying, "But I say to you, love your enemies" (v. 44). As we've already seen, Israel's religious brain trust had a hard time distinguishing between their neighbors and their enemies. That was essentially the issue that prompted the Lord to invent the parable of the good Samaritan.

Luke's gospel records that story of a scribe confronting Jesus, hoping to "put Him to the test" (Luke 10:25). He pointedly asked Christ how to inherit eternal life, and Christ prompted him to recite a variation on the first and second great commandments: "You shall love the LORD your God with all your heart, and with all your soul, and with all your strength, and with all your mind; and your neighbor as yourself" (v. 27). Christ replied, "You have answered correctly; do this and you will live" (v. 28), but the scribe wasn't satisfied. "Wishing to justify himself, he said to Jesus, 'And who is my neighbor?'" (v. 29).

The ensuing parable no doubt offended the sensibilities of Israel's religious leaders, and not just because the priest and the Levite in the story showed such casual uninterest in helping their fellow countryman who had been robbed, beaten, and left half-dead by the side of the road. The real offense came in the form of the parable's hero, a Samaritan whom all the Jews would have considered an avowed enemy. Christ's story not only exposed the haughty self-righteousness of the religious leaders, but it provoked their prejudices too. There were no ethnic or religious lines that excused Israel's animosity—anyone in their path with a need was to instantly become a potential object of their love.

In reality, Israel had been commanded in the Old Testament to treat both their neighbors and their enemies with the same kind of love. But Jesus, in classic rabbinical style reasoning from the greater to the lesser, immediately turned their attention to those hardest to love—those who were most offensive, objectionable, and distasteful. If you can faithfully love those kinds of people, you can love anyone.

It's worth noting that the love we are instructed to show to our enemies in Matthew 5:44 is not emotional but volitional. The Greek word here (*agapē*) speaks of the love of the will. It's not related to any personal fulfillment; rather, it is focused on acting for the other person's welfare and benefit. It's not interested in reciprocation. It is the love of unmitigated benevolence, prompted by a pure and invincible goodwill toward any needy person we encounter. Luke's gospel expands on Christ's words in Matthew 5, adding two practical applications of the love we are to show our enemies: "Do good to those who hate you, bless those who curse you" (Luke 6:27–28). One commentator captures the weight of the Lord's exhortation this way:

> [Love] indeed, sees all the hatefulness and the wickedness of the enemy, feels his stabs and his blows, may even have something to do toward warding them off; but all this simply fills the loving heart with the one desire and aim, to free its enemy from his hate, to rescue him from his sin, and thus to save his soul. Mere affection is often blind, but even then it thinks that it sees something attractive in the one toward whom it goes out; the higher love may see nothing attractive in the one so loved, . . . its inner motive is simply to bestow true blessing on the one loved, to do him the

highest good. . . . I cannot like a low, mean criminal who may have robbed me and threatened my life; I cannot like a false, lying, slanderous fellow who, perhaps, has vilified me again and again; but I can by the grace of Jesus Christ love them all, see what is wrong with them, desire and work to do them only good, most of all to free them from their vicious ways.[4]

After humbly stooping to wash the disciples' feet, Christ told them, "A new commandment I give to you, that you love one another, even as I have loved you" (John 13:34). Make no mistake—the disciples were not lovable men. In the years they spent with the Lord, they were quarrelsome, jealous, selfish, vindictive, and occasionally at odds with Christ Himself. Yet He perpetually put their needs above His own, loving them in spite of themselves. In the end, He laid down His life for them (15:13).

In the Sermon on the Mount, Christ commands that we show that same kind of love to our enemies.

Pray for Your Persecutors

Jesus' words become more intense as He continues: "Pray for those who persecute you" (Matt. 5:44). The Lord promised His disciples—and, by extension, all believers throughout the history of the church—that they would face persecution for His sake (John 15:20). In Matthew 5, He instructs us how to respond. He says to pray for those who are violent and hostile toward you. This is reminiscent of His statement at the end of the Beatitudes: "Blessed are those who have been persecuted for the sake of righteousness" (Matt. 5:10).

The Lord Himself exemplified this attitude on the cross when He said, "Father, forgive them; for they do not know what they are doing" (Luke 23:34). And God answered that prayer. He forgave one of the thieves (v. 43). He certainly forgave the centurion who was standing there (Matt. 27:54). And He forgave many people in that crowd, because they were regenerated on the day of Pentecost. In the agony of the cross, Christ was pleading with the Father for the sake of those who were inflicting His pain. That is how we are to desire the well-being of those who persecute us.

Stephen used one of his final breaths to cry out, "Lord, do not hold this sin against them!" (Acts 7:60). And who was standing right in front of him with the garments of the witnesses at his feet? Luke recorded that it was "a young man named Saul" (v. 58)—a man who devoted his life to the persecution of the early church, only to encounter the Lord on the road to Damascus and become an Apostle himself. God obviously answered Stephen's prayer on behalf of the Apostle Paul. In that sense, Paul was the *fruit* of Stephen's prayer. Stephen understood what it means to selflessly love those who persecute you, as he was praying to God for their forgiveness and redemption while they were still stoning him to death.

Again, we should hear the words of Bonhoeffer, who served as a pastor in Germany and was put to death by the Nazis. Regarding the command to love our enemies, he wrote: "This is the supreme demand. Through the medium of prayer we go to our enemy, stand by his side, and plead for him to God."[5] Faithfully praying for your persecutors is the noble high ground of godliness. Christ instructs us not just to forgo revenge but to petition Him on behalf of our oppressors and tormenters. Loving our enemies means pleading with God for their forgiveness and repentance.

Manifest Your Sonship

Commands don't always come with explanations. We're not always told *why* we're commanded to do something. But in Matthew 5:45, Jesus tells us why we are commanded to love our enemies and pray for our persecutors, and the reason points us to a glorious, climactic reality. He says, "So that you may be sons of your Father who is in heaven." This is an incredible statement. We demonstrate that we are children of God when we manifest His characteristics. How will the world know we truly belong to Him unless we love as He loves? And the more we behave in a godly manner, the more readily apparent it becomes that we are His children and possess His character.

Scripture is clear that our love is a powerful testimony to our sonship. The Lord told His disciples, "By this all men will know that you are My disciples, if you have love for one another" (John 13:35). In his first epistle, the Apostle John wrote, "God is love, and the one who abides in love abides in God, and God abides in him" (1 John 4:16). Moreover, he wrote, "If someone says, 'I love God,' and hates his brother, he is a liar; for the one who does not love his brother whom he has seen, cannot love

God whom he has not seen" (v. 20). Our love for others speaks volumes—particularly our love for the unlovable and for those who are unloving toward us.

In situations where we are confronted with the call to love our enemies, we need to remember that God loves His enemies too. While it's true the Lord's anger burns against the wicked and that He will one day pour out His wrath on the rebellious, at the same time, there is also a sense in which He shows His love to all mankind impartially. Theologians call this the doctrine of common grace, and we see examples of it in Scripture and throughout our daily lives. Psalm 145:15–16 highlights one example: "The eyes of all look to You, and You give them their food in due time. You open Your hand and satisfy the desire of every living thing." Put simply, God feeds everyone.

Christ gives us another illustration of God's common grace in the Sermon on the Mount. How do we know God loves everybody? Jesus says, "He causes His sun to rise on the evil and the good, and sends rain on the righteous and the unrighteous" (Matt. 5:45). God's common grace to all men is on display every day in His creation. To both the saved and the unsaved, He gives sunlight and rain to sustain life and grow food. He makes our lives possible. As Paul said in his sermon on Mars Hill, "In Him we live and move and exist" (Acts 17:28).

We can quickly touch on some other aspects of God's love that extend even to His enemies.[6] God loves the lost in that He holds back His wrath. In 1 Timothy 4:10, Paul refers to the Lord as "the Savior of all men, especially of believers." This isn't saying that all men will be spiritually and eternally saved;

rather, Paul has in mind the Lord's temporal protection of the lost against His immediate righteous judgment. Every breath an unregenerate person takes is another act of grace from a merciful, saving God. Not only that, but God also loves the lost in that He warns them of the judgment they will face unless they repent. In His Word and through His people, God is constantly calling sinners to turn from their ways and submit to Him in faith. Jesus put it this way: "The one who comes to Me I will certainly not cast out" (John 6:37). We have the privilege of extending God's love to the lost by calling them to repentance and faith.

We also see God's love for the lost in His compassion. Scripture is clear that God is grieved by the perversion of His image in man's rebellion and by the eternal consequences of unrepentant sin. Luke 19:41 tells us Christ wept for Jerusalem. Matthew recorded the Lord's lament over the city: "Jerusalem, Jerusalem, who kills the prophets and stones those who are sent to her! How often I wanted to gather your children together, the way a hen gathers her chicks under her wings, and you were unwilling. Behold, your house is being left to you desolate! For I say to you, from now on you will not see Me until you say, 'Blessed is He who comes in the name of the LORD!' " (23:37–39). Our God has great compassion for the lost. We must cultivate the same kind of compassion for the sinners in our midst, spurring us on to proclaim His truth.

That's the love of God that extends to everyone, and the kind of love we must show to others if we're going to be identified as His children. This love is not limited to some narrow definition of who qualifies as your neighbor, as the Jews had done. It's not limited to only the people you happen to like or the people who naturally attract your affection. It extends even to people who hate you and those who would wound, defraud, and persecute you. It extends to people who are outside your social circles—even to those on the fringes of society. And it's not just for your family and friends. Christ points out that even rank sinners and pagans can show affection for loved ones (Matt. 5:46–47).

Jesus is saying that there is a love of God that extends beyond His love for His own. God loves even His enemies—those who hate Him, those who hated His Son, and those who persecute His people to this day.

And if we are going to be known as our Father's children, we need to manifest that same kind of love for the lost. He demonstrates His love to sinners through general goodness, pity, warning, admonition, real grief over their plight, and a pleading offer of the saving gospel. We must love our neighbors—*including our enemies*—in the same way. We need to prioritize their general welfare. If that means a meal, clothing, money, or some other kind of assistance, we give it freely, out of a sincere desire for their good. More than that, we show them pity, compassion, and grief over their slavery to sin and the consequences that await if they do not repent. Loving our enemies also means warning them of God's judgment and faithfully, lovingly admonishing them to repent and believe while there is still time. That is loving our neighbors the way God loves.

Christ's words in Matthew 5:48 tell us what we likely already know: that such perfect love is impossible on our own. He says, "Therefore you are to be perfect, as your heavenly Father is perfect." The point of the Sermon on the Mount was to expose the futility of the Jews' self-righteous religion. Over and over, sinful man is confronted with his inability to meet God's standard on his own terms. Holiness and righteousness are beyond our reach.

But the point is not to send us into despair. Rather, it's to drive us into the arms of our Savior. It's to burn the truth of Matthew 19:26 into our minds—that "with people this is impossible, but with God all things are possible." Even as new creations in Christ, we constantly need to be reminded not to rely on ourselves—to push aside the pride and self-righteousness that come so easy to us all. We need to recognize the weakness of our flesh and cast ourselves onto the mercy and strength of our Lord.

And as He sheds His love abroad in our hearts, may we learn to share it faithfully—not only with our fellow believers and others who are easy to love, but with all our neighbors, and particularly those who are difficult to love, and even those who qualify as our enemies. May the Lord soften our hearts for the people He's placed in our midst, and may we be mindful that we were once His enemies and would still be if it weren't for His great love.

Chapter Three

THE CHRISTIAN LIFE MEANS LOVING UNTIL IT HURTS

The world talks a lot about love. But the more people talk about it, the less it seems as if they actually know what they're talking about. They certainly don't seem to understand what divine love is or how it functions.

Worse still, the same kind of confusion is creeping into the church. For example, you have probably heard some pastor or some church describe their desire to "just love on people." That sounds good, but often it doesn't actually mean anything beyond the superficial. Increasingly, what it actually means is, "We don't want to make people uncomfortable." Churches like that routinely settle for a vague sense of acceptance that's not grounded in any biblical truth. They inevitably skirt the difficult topics and the penetrating and convicting truths, instead planting their flags in whatever inoffensive common ground they can identify. They've mastered the technique of sounding loving without having to say anything of substance.

That's not love; it's pacification. Real love—the kind we ought to be cultivating in the church—has nothing to do with ignorant sentimentality, false peace, superficial emotions, or fickle affections. Love, in its highest and purest form, doesn't settle for momentary happiness or a shallow sense of unity. Real love isn't interested in temporary satisfaction; it has eternal goals in mind. It's concerned with another person's well-being, godliness, and spiritual growth. In fact, love is willing to confront when necessary—it will risk alienating the other person's affection for the sake of his ultimate spiritual good. And real love doesn't fret over the temporal cost—it's ready to expend itself for the good of the believer and the glory of God.

Real love means being willing to love until it hurts.

Sacrificial Love

First of all, loving until it hurts means loving others enough to serve them sacrificially. We find a vivid example of this kind of love in John 13, during one of the Lord's most memorable interactions with His disciples. As was their usual pastime, the disciples had been arguing about which of them would be the greatest in the kingdom of God. In spite of their intimate relationship with Christ and the front-row seat they had throughout His public ministry, they were often preoccupied with their own well-being, prosperity, and future. In fact, James and John had the unmitigated audacity to send their mother to Jesus, asking if they could sit at His right and left hand in the kingdom (Matt. 20:20–21). The rest of the disciples were furious (v. 24)—not because this was some breach of spiritual integrity, but because they were being crowded out by the request. In that instance, Christ warned them about the trials He would soon endure, explaining to them that He had come "to give His life a ransom for many" (v. 28). But the disciples were indifferent to His words—they continued to jockey for position in the kingdom, right up to the night of Christ's betrayal and arrest (Luke 22:24).

That's the scene as we approach the upper room in John 13:1. At the end of the verse, we read, "Having loved His own who were in the world, He loved them to the end." Amazingly, this sovereign, saving, keeping, eternal God reached beyond the disciples' ugliness, selfishness, indifference, pride, and preoccupation with their own ambitions and loved them without limit. That is the first point John established in chapter 13. Christ loved them to the fullest, to the absolute maximum of His divine capacity.

The passage goes on to illustrate how Jesus displayed that love. John writes: "Jesus, knowing that the Father had given all things into His hands, and that He had come forth from God and was going back to God, got up from supper, and laid aside His garments; and taking a towel, He girded Himself. Then He poured water into the basin, and began to wash the disciples' feet and to wipe them with the towel with which He was girded" (vv. 3–5).

Some background is helpful for comprehending the gravity of the humble, loving service Christ provided. In the Jewish culture of the day, it was customary to engage in foot washing anytime there was a meal like this one. The people wore sandals, and the dusty, muddy roads kept their feet dirty. Beyond that, meals like this tended to be a prolonged experience. People did not quickly stop by and then leave for another activity but often spent three or four hours together. Dinners of this kind could encompass the whole evening. And typically, they would sit not upright in hard chairs but instead reclined in a comfortable position, putting them in close proximity with another guest's feet. So as a common courtesy, there was a servant—usually the lowliest slave in the household—whose responsibility it was to wash all the dinner guests' feet.

On this particular evening, no servant had been provided to do the foot washing. One thing was sure: the disciples were not going to do it, because none of them wanted to take on the humiliation. In spite of the years spent together in brotherhood, each of them apparently believed he was above the level of one who would stoop to perform this common courtesy for the others. Understanding that none of them would undertake this very obvious and necessary task, the Lord took it upon Himself. The Son of God stood up from the table, retrieved the necessary implements, and humbly began to wash the disciples' feet.

Scripture records Peter's response, which was likely indicative of how the others reacted. "He said to Him, 'Lord, do You wash my feet?' Jesus answered and said to him, 'What I do you do not realize now, but you will understand hereafter' " (John 13:6–7). Peter couldn't appreciate the gravity of what was happening; none of them could. Christ was demonstrating His humility—not merely as one Man washing another's feet but as the Lord and Creator of the universe who had come to seek and save the lost. It's the same kind of humility the Apostle Paul described in his letter to the Philippians: "Have this attitude in yourselves which was also in Christ Jesus, who, although He existed in the form of God, did not regard equality with God a thing to be grasped, but emptied Himself, taking the form of a bond-servant, and being made in the likeness of men. Being found in appearance as a man, He humbled Himself by becoming obedient to the point of death, even death on a cross" (Phil. 2:5–8). Washing His disciples' feet was an outward manifestation of the humiliation Christ had already endured and would continue to endure all the way to the cross.

Few people have the audacity to command the sovereign Lord of heaven, but Peter was one of them. He had no compunctions about telling the Lord exactly what He should do. "Peter said to Him, 'Never shall You wash my feet!' Jesus answered him, 'If I do not wash you, you have no part with Me' " (John 13:8).

When the impetuous disciple realized that it might jeopardize his relationship with Jesus, he quickly changed his mind. "Simon Peter said to Him, 'Lord, then wash not only my feet, but also my hands and my head.' Jesus said to him, 'He who has bathed needs only to wash his feet, but is completely clean; and you are clean, but not all of you' " (vv. 9–10). You wouldn't take a full bath every time your hands or feet get dirty. In the same way, believers don't require the complete cleansing and regeneration of the new birth every time they sin. Once the righteousness of Christ has been imputed to us (2 Cor. 5:21), we need only the washing of the Spirit's sanctifying work that goes on throughout the believer's life.

However, Jesus noted that not all of them were clean; He singled out Judas by implication: "For He knew the one who was betraying Him; for this reason He said, 'Not all of you are clean' " (John 13:11). Jesus knew the hearts of His disciples. He knew Peter's impulsive passions and that His beloved disciple would deny Him three times later that evening (v. 38). In the same way, He knew that Judas would soon betray Him and that even as he sat at the table, his heart already belonged to Satan. And yet, Jesus stooped to wash His betrayer's feet too.

John's account of that evening in the upper room continues:

> When He had washed their feet, and taken His garments and reclined at the table again, He said to them, "Do you know what I have done to you? You call Me Teacher and Lord; and you are right, for so I am. If I then, the Lord and the Teacher, washed your feet, you also ought to wash one another's feet. For I gave you an example that you also should do as I did to you. Truly, truly, I say to you, a slave is not greater than his master, nor is one who is sent greater than the one who sent him." (vv. 12–16)

In other words, Jesus was telling them, "If you're not willing to get down and do the most abject kind of service on behalf of someone else, if you're not willing to take on the lowest role of a slave and wash someone else's feet, then you are effectively saying you are superior to Me." Christ's words would have pierced their consciences. They should pierce ours as well. Do we readily humble ourselves to meet the needs of others? Or do we harbor the prideful notion that we're above that kind of service—that someone else will take care of it? Jesus made it clear that if we think we're too good to serve others, what we're really saying is that we're better than Him.

On the other hand, our readiness to humbly serve and lovingly sacrifice is a testimony to our Savior. Christ Himself makes that point explicit: "A new commandment I give to you, that you love one another, even as I have loved you, that you also love one another. By this all men will know that you are My disciples, if you have love for one another" (John 13:34–35). We need to follow the example of Jesus and be willing to set aside our prominence and pride to serve sacrificially those we see in need. Loving until it hurts means sacrificing yourself for the sake of others.

Jesus summed up the relationship between love and sacrifice in His monumental statement "Greater love has no one than this, that one lay down his life for his friends" (John 15.13). Loving and serving others may require the ultimate sacrifice. In Philippians 2:17, Paul wrote, "But even if I am being poured out as a drink offering upon the sacrifice and service of your faith, I rejoice and share my joy with you all." Paul served Christ by serving His church, and it cost him his life. In his epistle to the Galatians, he says, "I bear on my body the marks of Jesus" (Gal. 6:17, ESV). All the scars that were inflicted on him throughout his ministry—scars from whips, rods, stones, stocks, and who knows what else—were all badges of Paul's sacrificial service. They marked him as a man who literally gave up his life for other people.

We need to cultivate that same humility and willingness to expend and sacrifice ourselves for others. We must be ready to give up our time, our priorities, our social standing, our comfort, and even our lives in care for others. When we see people who need their proverbial feet washed, we should leap at the opportunity. Loving until it hurts means loving others enough to sacrifice everything we have—including ourselves.

Sanctifying Love

We turn to another pivotal moment between Christ and His disciples for a second example of loving until it hurts. The Lord's words in Matthew 18 show us that our love must be not only sacrificial but also sanctifying.

Matthew 18 is a powerful chapter, worthy of careful attention. Portions of this chapter, of course, are very familiar to us. We have heard about becoming like children to enter the kingdom. We know what to do if our hand or foot causes us to stumble. We remember the story about the man with a hundred sheep and the one that went astray. We've read Christ's words about rebuking a sinning brother, the conversation with Peter about forgiving seventy times seven, and the convicting parable about the man who was forgiven much but refused to forgive little. These are all familiar to us, but there is a tendency for them to become disconnected and disjointed and therefore misunderstood.

Before examining the passage more closely, let's consider the larger context of the book. The gospel of Matthew features the greatest sermons ever preached by Jesus. The first and most familiar is called the Sermon on the Mount (Matt. 5–7), which exposes the apostate religion that dominated Judaism at the time. Some have mistaken the Sermon on the Mount for a simple treatise on Christian ethics, but it's much more than that. It's a message that identifies man's inability to achieve God's holy standard. It's a gospel call to lead people from the false religion of works-righteousness to their true need for God's grace.

Moving forward through the gospel of Matthew, the Lord identifies His disciples and then launches into a sermon on the topic of discipleship in chapter 10. In chapter 13, we encounter His monumental sermon on the parables of the kingdom, designed to help His disciples and us understand the character of the age in which we do gospel ministry. Matthew chapter 23 contains a most notable diatribe—a condemning sermon against the religious leaders of Israel, in which Jesus calls them "blind guides" (v. 16) and "whitewashed tombs" (v. 27). That sermon, preached on the grounds of the temple, was Christ's fiercest denunciation of Israel's religious elite. Finally, we come to chapters 24 and 25 of Matthew's gospel, containing the Lord's sermon on His second coming, called the Olivet Discourse, because it was delivered on the side of the Mount of Olives.

In the midst of those landmark sermons, we can lose sight of Matthew 18, which is a crucial sermon on God's love for His people and the priority He places on their purity. It's a portrait of the sanctifying love that should be evident among God's people—love that builds up, that takes sin seriously, that loves and protects the body of Christ, and that, when necessary, confronts the sin in its midst.

The Childlikeness of Believers

The scene begins when the disciples are again arguing about who is the greatest in the kingdom. Verse 1 says, "At that time the disciples came to Jesus and said, 'Who then is the greatest in the kingdom of heaven?' " They expected Him to identify one of them, but Jesus used their infighting and pride to teach them a lesson. These events likely took place in Capernaum—it might have even been in Peter's own house. Matthew records that Jesus "called a child to Himself and set him before them, and said, 'Truly I say to you, unless you are converted and become like children, you will not enter the kingdom of heaven' " (vv. 2–3). As usual, the disciples were indulging their pride, looking forward to the prominence and exaltation they expected to enjoy in Christ's kingdom. Instead, Jesus stunned them by saying that they would not even *enter* His kingdom unless they became like children.

What was Jesus saying? Simply this: little children have achieved nothing. They give nothing and they do nothing; they just make demands. They have no accomplishments to point to or credentials to tout. They are utterly incapable of survival on their own, thus totally dependent. In the same sense, the kingdom of heaven is not all about how much you have achieved; rather, it's about knowing what you *cannot* achieve. In fact, if your eyes are trained on your accomplishments, your greatness, and your exaltation, there is no place for you in Christ's kingdom to begin with.

The Lord continues in verse 4, "Whoever then humbles himself as this child, he is the greatest in the kingdom of heaven." He says the greatest is the most humble. That must have sent ripples of shocked embarrassment through the crowd. These grown men should have been shamed out of their endless pursuit of preeminence, but we've already seen that this trend continued virtually all the way to the cross.

Verse 5 turns an important corner: "And whoever receives one such child in My name receives Me." Note that Jesus is not talking about physical infants in this verse; He's talking about spiritual children—believers—who are the children of the kingdom of heaven. And we must recognize that all the other children in the kingdom, all our brothers and sisters in Christ, are one with Christ. In fact, Jesus says in Matthew 25:40, "Truly I say to you, to the extent that you did it to one of these brothers of Mine, even the least of them, you did it to Me." Therefore, how we treat other believers is how we treat Christ, as He is perpetually present in them. Showing sanctifying love to one another in God's family means we recognize Christ in each other, and that we love and serve one another accordingly.

Taking Sin Seriously

But it's not just about a brotherly reception; Christ commands us to *protect* each other as well. "Whoever causes one of these little ones who believe in Me to stumble, it would be better for him to have a heavy millstone hung around his neck, and to be drowned in the depth of the sea" (Matt. 18:6). Again, Jesus is not talking about actual children; He's referring to believers. And what does it mean to cause them to stumble? It means to trip them up and cause them to fall into sin, either by direct solicitation or indirectly by pushing their buttons to evoke a sinful response. It's also possible to cause another believer to stumble simply by setting a bad example. It could also be through the misuse of your liberty in Christ that you lead another Christian into sin. Or it could be a simple sin of omission—by failing to do what is right, you could encourage others to show the same careless disregard on that point of obedience. Regardless of how it happens, we need to appreciate the danger of leading God's children into sin. Jesus says it would be better for us to be horrifically drowned.

To put it another way, Christ is commanding us to prioritize the purity and holiness of His people. We need to love one another in a way that protects and promotes sanctification. Rather than causing each other to stumble, we work to build one another up in godliness and love for the truth.

We also need to avoid the world's attempts to inhibit our growth in godliness. In verse 7, Jesus says, "Woe to the world because of its stumbling blocks!" God's children need to be aware of the stumbling blocks the world will hurl into our paths. We need to watch out for the world's attempts to seduce us with what 1 John 2:16 describes as "the lust of the flesh and the lust of the eyes and the boastful pride of life." We expect the world to be a solicitor for wickedness and to do anything and everything to seduce believers away from obedience to God. As Christ says, "For it is inevitable that stumbling blocks come; but woe to that man through whom the stumbling block comes!" (Matt. 18:7). God keeps detailed accounts, even with the world, and judgment will fall on those who seduce His children and stifle their spiritual growth.

In verses 8 and 9, the Lord delivers His graphic exhortation for believers to remove the stumbling blocks from their own lives. He says: "If your hand or your foot causes you to stumble, cut it off and throw it from you; it is better for you to enter life crippled or lame, than to have two hands or two feet and be cast into the eternal fire. If your eye causes you to stumble, pluck it out and throw it from you. It is better for you to enter life with one eye, than to have two eyes and be cast into the fiery hell." Jesus is not commanding actual physical dismemberment here; literally cutting off a limb or plucking out an eye would not correct anything in the heart. Instead, He's explaining that sin is so serious it must be dealt with drastically and thoroughly. It's a dramatic way to say, "Deal with your sin before it leads to destruction."

Sanctifying love takes sin seriously. It refuses to toy with temptation in our own hearts or to carelessly lead other believers into sin and rebellion.

God's Pursuit of His People

After establishing the priority of purity, Jesus circles back to God's love for His children in verse 10. He says, "See that you do not despise one of these little ones, for I say to you that their angels in heaven continually see the face of My Father who is in heaven." The idea here is that we are not to look down on God's people or think of them as inferior to ourselves. Partiality has no place in the household of God—we should not be attempting to one-up or outdo each other. This rebuke was particularly poignant for the disciples, who had just been arguing over their own positions in the kingdom. Their incessant ambition only served to belittle their fellow disciples, stoking their jealousy and stirring up resentment in their ranks. Instead of desiring elevated honor, they should have been building up each other.

In the same way, we must be careful how we treat God's beloved children, because all heaven is preoccupied with their care. The Father is looking at His children, and the angels are watching the face of the Father so that they can immediately be dispatched to the aid of that believer. We need to realize there is a heavenly audience always observing our dealings with one another. When we're tempted to think no one else is looking, we need to remember the accountability we have in heaven. God is paying close attention to how His children treat each other.

And what happens when one of them wanders away? Matthew records a familiar parable from Christ: "If any man has a hundred sheep, and one of them has gone astray, does he not leave the ninety-nine on the mountains and go and search for the one that is straying?" (v. 12). When a child disappears, the rest of the family frantically scours the house, the block, and the neighborhood until they find him. But in the church, we often fail to show the same care and concern for our spiritual family. When someone leaves the church, we can be tempted to think: "Well, he was always a problem. He never quite got it. It's probably a good thing he moved on to another church." We cannot think so dismissively about God's children. We need to show the same passionate care and concern that their heavenly Father shows for them—the same He shows for us, as well. That's one of the reasons why large churches must work hard to integrate new people into small groups, so that they're not just nameless faces in the crowd. We need to be diligent in getting to know the fellow believers God has placed in our midst—to know where they are spiritually and know what's going on in their lives in order to better support and stimulate their spiritual growth.

God didn't save us and call us into His eternal family just to have us wander aimlessly, surviving on inconsistent spiritual sustenance and never belonging to a local church body. Such meandering is dangerous to our spiritual growth. As Jesus explains in verse 14, "It is not the will of your Father who is in heaven that one of these little ones perish." In this context, "perish" is not referring to death or destruction. Rather, it's a reference to the way falling into sin destroys the believer's usefulness to the work of the kingdom. It also corrupts his relationships, primarily with God but also with other believers.

Showing sanctifying love means that, like God, we are grieved when believers fall into sin—and that we rejoice along with Him when the stray sheep is brought home (v. 13).

The Love That Disciplines

Sanctifying love also includes a willingness to confront those brothers and sisters who fall into sin. In this next portion of His sermon, the Lord lays out His specific and detailed pattern for dealing with sin in the church. These instructions don't give us license to pounce on people for making a small error or carelessly saying something they shouldn't. Love covers those kinds of sins, or at least it's supposed to. What Christ is prescribing here is a means to address patterns of sin that are destructive to the believer's own life or a threat to infect and pollute the rest of the church. The point of this process is not to kick problem people out of the church. It's to restore the sinning brother to a right relationship with God and believers, so as to protect the integrity of the church and its testimony to the watching world.

Jesus says, "If your brother sins, go and show him his fault in private; if he listens to you, you have won your brother" (v. 15). Church discipline is a series of steps—the first is done in private. In a sense, this step is preliminary to the process. We should be faithful to lovingly confront sin where we see it in the lives of the believers around us. If God's people were more faithful in addressing sin when it first appeared—if they didn't turn a blind eye and hope the problem went away on its own—there would be fewer instances that demanded the subsequent steps in the process. We need to love each other enough to confront the sin that stifles our fellow believer's spiritual growth and stunts his usefulness to God's kingdom. And if he responds positively to such loving confrontation, there is no need to go beyond that. Christ says, "You have won your brother." By God's grace, we rejoice in His goodness and in the repentance His Spirit has produced.

However, not everyone will repent, regardless of how sincere or compelling that first confrontation was. In those cases, Jesus says, "But if he does not listen to you, take one or two more with you, so that by the mouth of two or three witnesses every fact may be confirmed" (v. 16). Sanctifying love does not easily lose heart; it persists for the sake of the sinning brother. We confront him again and plead with him to repent, taking witnesses to give testimony to his response. Again, the hope here is to help the wayward believer see his sin the way God sees it and deal with it directly.

"If he refuses to listen to them," Christ says, "tell it to the church" (v. 17). It's a sober thing to bring the sins of a believer before the whole church body. This isn't an act of sanctified gossip. We urge the rest of the church to pursue the unrepentant person in love, calling him back to faithfulness to Christ. "And if he refuses to listen even to the church, let him be to you as a Gentile and a tax collector" (v. 17). If he won't submit and repent after unleashing the entire church on him, at that point the church is forced to treat him as an unbeliever, because he is behaving like one. If he's living in open, unrepentant sin, there is nothing to certify him as a believer.

It's no small thing to put somebody out of the church, but you do it out of love for him. Paul tells us that the unrepentant sinner might have to suffer "the destruction of his flesh, so that his spirit may be saved in the day of the Lord Jesus" (1 Cor. 5:5). The Lord may take him out of the world altogether to bring an end to his sin and remove the stain on the testimony of His church. But the hope is that disassociating the unrepentant sinner from the blessedness of fellowship will get his attention in a way the prior confrontations did not.

That said, you also put him out of the church out of love for the rest of the body. He cannot be allowed to stay within the fellowship, because "a little leaven leavens the whole lump of dough" (1 Cor. 5:6). His sin could fester and spread throughout the church like a cancer. In this regard, sanctifying love prioritizes both the one who is in sin and the rest of the church.

A common argument against church discipline is that no one will want to join a congregation that practices it. However, the transformed heart has holy longings. The world is aggressively wicked, and regenerate believers are eager to belong to a church body that emphasizes holiness, integrity, and sanctification. It's true that a church full of judgmental busybodies with Sequoia-sized logs in their own eyes won't attract anyone. But that's not true church discipline. God wants us to keep His church pure, starting with our own lives. A truly disciplined church is one where all its members are continually taking inventory of their own hearts before rushing to confront the sin they spot in others. Sanctifying love keeps careful watch over one's own heart, first of all.

And if the church is forced to go through the entire process of church discipline and put a member out of the church, what confidence do we have that it was what God wanted? The Lord says, "Truly I say to you, whatever you bind on earth shall have been bound in heaven; and whatever you loose on earth shall have been loosed in heaven. Again I say to you, that if two of you agree on earth about anything that they may ask, it shall be done for them by My Father who is in heaven" (Matt. 18:18–19). Christ is confirming the church's authority to conduct such discipline. If we confront a sinning believer and he does not repent, we can say he is bound in his sin because that's what the Bible says. If he does repent, we can say he is loosed from his sin because that's what the Bible says. In other words, we are doing on earth what heaven has already done. We are rendering a verdict consistent with the verdict that heaven has already rendered.

Moreover, Christ confirms His participation in the process, saying, "For where two or three have gathered together in My name, I am there in their midst" (v. 20). In the first chapter of Revelation, the Apostle John received a vision illustrating Christ's relationship to His church. John wrote: "His eyes were like a flame of fire. His feet were like burnished bronze, when it has been made to glow in a furnace" (Rev. 1:14–15). This is a picture of Christ's purifying work—work that He accomplishes in part through the process of church discipline. In that sense, our sanctifying love for other believers is a reflection of the Lord's, as He desires the church to be His holy, spotless bride.

With the Lord's sermon in Matthew 18 coming to a close, Peter wondered aloud: "Lord, how often shall my brother sin against me and I forgive him? Up to seven times?" (v. 21). In those days, the rabbis instructed that forgiveness was only to be offered three times. Perhaps Peter thought if he doubled that and added one, the Lord would be impressed. But Christ's reply deflated those hopes. He said, "I do not say to you, up to seven times, but up to seventy times seven" (v. 22), meaning endlessly. Believers are never more like God than when they forgive, and Christ is describing the magnanimous, gracious, endless forgiveness we receive from the Father. He closes the sermon with a familiar parable illustrating that very point (vv. 23–35).

But if such forgiveness is not coupled with the confrontation of sin, evil will find a comfortable seat in the church. We need to forgive one another freely, out of godly love and the recognition of what we've already been forgiven in Christ. But we also need to faithfully confront those sinning believers out of a sanctifying love, both for the sake of their spiritual growth and to preserve the purity of the church for the honor of the Lord.

Suffering Love

We've seen that loving until it hurts means loving enough to sacrifice and loving enough to sanctify. Finally, it also means loving enough to suffer. We already touched on the physical suffering that marked Paul's ministry. But the fiercest suffering he endured didn't come from a whip or a stone—it came from the people he served. Paul's physical pain didn't come close to the concerns he bore for those churches. And no church was a greater concern than the church at Corinth.

The Corinthians were a source of endless suffering for Paul. They followed false teachers. They mutinied and rebelled against him. And they believed terrible lies about him. When he visited the church, a man in the congregation stood up and accused him to his face, and nobody came to his defense (see 2 Cor. 2:5–8, 10). He left town broken and shattered, his love for them unrequited. He was so distressed by the Corinthians that he said he was depressed (7:6). He was emotionally battered and bruised by these people.

Paul's relationship with the Corinthians is a good reminder that the more you love somebody, the more you put yourself at risk to be hurt. He made that very point in 2 Corinthians 12:15 when he wrote: "I will most gladly spend and be expended for your souls. If I love you more, am I to be loved less?" Sadly, that's a common pattern, and it could happen to any of us. The more we love someone, the less they may love us in return.

In Paul's case, the more he loved them, the more he spoke straight to them and their sin. We only have the two inspired letters of Paul to the Corinthians. He had written them a letter before 1 Corinthians that is not in the canon of Scripture, and then he wrote 1 Corinthians, which was a very confrontational letter. After that, he wrote another letter before 2 Corinthians that is not in the canon either. This is often referred to as the "severe letter" (see 2 Cor. 2:4; 7:8–9), and it was a confrontation about their defection to the false teachers. Then he was prompted by the Holy Spirit to write 2 Corinthians, again to deal with their spiritual defection and to reassert the genuineness of his Apostolic office. Over and over in the two inspired epistles that we have, we see how these people had cut him to the heart and left deep wounds.

In fact, I believe that's what Paul was referring to when he described the thorn in his flesh. He wrote, "Because of the surpassing greatness of the revelations, for this reason, to keep me from exalting myself, there was given me a thorn in the flesh, a messenger of Satan to torment me—to keep me from exalting myself!" (2 Cor. 12:7). There are an endless number of speculative theories about what the thorn in the flesh actually was. People wonder, Was it eye disease? Was it malaria? Was it his mother-in-law? I don't think it was meant to be that complex or confusing. Paul himself said the thorn in the flesh was "a messenger of Satan." The Greek word translated as "messenger" is *angelos*, which the New Testament commonly uses to refer to angels. And an angel of Satan is a demon. Therefore, Paul was saying that a demon had come into the false teachers, brought them into the Corinthian church, and shredded that congregation. It turned the people against Paul and true doctrine. Though their rejection and rebellion were crushing to him, the Lord allowed this deep suffering because it humbled the Apostle. It is amazing the degree to which the Lord will go to humble His servant.

We talk about it as Paul's "thorn in the flesh," but the Greek word (*skolops*) could be more accurately translated as "stake." Paul was not talking about some minor external irritation.

The demonic influence on the Corinthians had driven a stake through his heart. He was impaled in agony over what was happening in that church. He had loved them, and what he received in return was hostility and anger because they did not want to face their sins.

That is what it means to love until it hurts. It means we are willing to serve sacrificially, to sanctify, and to suffer. We can expect pain in this degree of love for others. But it is a glorious pain, because God uses it to refine us into His image and sharpen us for the work of His kingdom.

- Chapter Four -

THE CHRISTIAN LIFE MEANS ENGAGING IN PRAYER

The New Testament is clear that God's people are to be people of prayer. Christ instructed His disciples, "Keep watching and praying that you may not enter into temptation" (Matt. 26:41). Luke described one encounter with the disciples in which "He was telling them a parable to show that at all times they ought to pray and not to lose heart" (Luke 18:1). Paul instructed his readers to be "devoted to prayer" (Rom. 12:12), to "pray at all times" (Eph. 6:18), and to "pray without ceasing" (1 Thess. 5:17). In Philippians 4:6, he wrote, "Be anxious for nothing, but in everything by prayer and supplication with thanksgiving let your requests be made known to God."

In response to those and other biblical exhortations to pray, the natural question is, How should we pray? Perhaps the best answer to that question is another one: How did the Lord teach us to pray?

For that answer, we turn to Christ's instructions in Luke 11:1–4.

It happened that while Jesus was praying in a certain place, after He had finished, one of His disciples said to Him, "Lord, teach us to pray just as John also taught his disciples." And He said to them, "When you pray, say:

'Father, hallowed be Your name.
Your kingdom come.
'Give us each day our daily bread.
'And forgive us our sins,
For we ourselves also forgive everyone who is
    indebted to us.
And lead us not into temptation.' "

Cultural Context

Some background is helpful in our quest to understand this passage. The notion of personal access to God Himself, on an intimate level, was an alien idea to the Jews in Jesus' day. They had been taught by the rabbis that God was far off. They believed their Creator was so transcendent that they could not truly experience any kind of intimate fellowship with Him. At Mount Sinai, the Israelites had witnessed the presence of God, accompanied by frightening displays of thunder, lightning, and smoke. They saw then what the writer of Hebrews later put into words—that "our God is a consuming fire" (12:29). No one could actually enter His presence except the high priest once every year, on the Day of Atonement—and even then, only after a lengthy process of cleansing and preparation. By the time of our Lord, God was widely seen as frighteningly unapproachable. The Jews would not even speak His name.

However, looking back at the Old Testament, it is abundantly clear that God did not reveal Himself in such an impersonal way. Over and over, we see that He commanded His people to approach Him in prayer—that He welcomed it. Psalm 50:15 says, "Call upon Me in the day of trouble; I shall rescue you, and you will honor Me." Psalm 91:15 echoes that idea, saying, "He will call upon Me, and I will answer him." Psalm 145:18 explains, "The LORD is near to all who call upon Him." Psalm 65:2 refers to God as "O You who hear prayer, to You all men come." And in Psalm 18:6, David recounted, "In my distress I called upon the LORD, and cried to my God for help; He heard my voice out of His temple, and my cry for help before Him came into His ears."

There's more. Proverbs 15 tells us, "The prayer of the upright is His delight" (v. 8) and "He hears the prayer of the righteous" (v. 29). The Old Testament also recounts many of the specific prayers God heard from His people. Hannah begged God for a son (1 Sam. 1:10–11) and poured out a heart of thanksgiving when He granted her request (2:1–10). Elijah prayed for God to resurrect the widow's son (1 Kings 17:21). Hezekiah prayed for healing (2 Kings 20:2–3). And "from the stomach of the fish," Jonah pleaded with God for forgiveness and deliverance

(Jonah 2:1–9). The presence of God was at the heart of life in the Old Testament. He was always near to His people, available to hear their petitions, and intimately involved in their lives.

When we analyze the components of the prayers of the people of God in the Old Testament, some key themes emerge. For example, Jewish prayers emphasized love and praise for God. Psalm 34:1 says, "I will bless the LORD at all times; His praise shall continually be in my mouth." In Psalm 51:15 we read David's plea, "O Lord, open my lips, that my mouth may declare Your praise." Closely related to those expressions of love and praise are the themes of gratitude and thanksgiving. Jonah 2:9 says, "I will sacrifice to You with the voice of thanksgiving." Some rabbis taught that thanksgiving was an essential element for every prayer.

Old Testament prayers also included a recognition and affirmation of God's holiness. In 1 Samuel 2:2, Hannah exulted, "There is no one holy like the LORD, indeed, there is no one besides You, nor is there any rock like our God." Prayer was an opportunity to celebrate the goodness of God's law and His commandments, along with expressing one's eagerness to obey them. The psalmist said, "Let my tongue sing of Your word, for all Your commandments are righteous" (Ps. 119:172).

Confession was another cornerstone of Old Testament prayer, often coupled with longings for a pure heart. Psalm 26:6 says, "I shall wash my hands in innocence, and I will go about Your altar, O LORD." David asked: "Who may ascend into the hill of the LORD? And who may stand in His holy place? He who has clean hands and a pure heart" (Ps. 24:3–4).

Moses interceded with God on behalf of the rebellious Israelites (Num. 14:13–19). In the same way, Ezra (Ezra 9:5–15), Nehemiah (Neh. 1:4–11), and Daniel (Dan. 9:3–19) offered prayers of corporate repentance on behalf of God's people.

One other noteworthy hallmark of Old Testament prayers was humility. Jews often began their prayers with the phrase "May it be Thy good pleasure." David expressed the humility of his heart with these words: "O LORD, my heart is not proud, nor my eyes haughty; nor do I involve myself in great matters, or in things too difficult for me" (Ps. 131:1). And although her prayer is recorded in the New Testament, Mary's reaction to the news that she would give birth to the Son of God exemplifies the humble perspective God's people have of themselves and their worthiness: "My soul exalts the Lord, and my spirit has rejoiced in God my Savior. For He has had regard for the humble state of His bondslave; for behold, from this time on all generations will count me blessed. For the Mighty One has done great things for me; and holy is His name" (Luke 1:46–49).

As you can see, prayer in the Old Testament followed essentially the same structure and reflected the same emphases that the Lord prescribed to His disciples. And that's why this brief background is important—it shows that Jesus was not giving them radically new instructions. All the elements we find in the exemplary prayers throughout Israel's history are emphasized and refined by our Lord in His instructions. He was essentially reestablishing the pattern that had been lost over the years, further illustrating that He came not to overturn or replace but to fulfill.

Teach Us to Pray

Our text in Luke 11 is similar to instructions the Lord gave His disciples in Matthew 6:9–13, but they are not records of the same incident. The Matthew account occurred in Galilee, while the event Luke described happened months later in Judea. Jesus was repeating instructions He likely gave at other times throughout His ministry. And in this instance, He was prompted by a request from one of His disciples. "It happened that while Jesus was praying in a certain place, after He had finished, one of His disciples said to Him, 'Lord, teach us to pray just as John also taught his disciples' " (Luke 11:1).

We don't know exactly where this exchange took place. Luke simply tells us that Jesus had been praying, and after He finished, the disciples initiated this conversation. Constant communication with His Father was a regular part of our Lord's life, and there is no doubt that the disciples had this experience with Him many times. While He often prayed alone, privacy was not always possible. On this occasion, the disciples may have been watching and listening, wondering about the structure or the nature of His prayers.

As though Christ needed persuading, they even brought up the fact that John the Baptist had taught his disciples how to pray. The scribes and Pharisees also acknowledged that "the disciples of John often fast and offer prayers" (Luke 5:33) and tried to use that fact to shame Christ and His disciples. In this case, it seems Christ's disciples simply didn't want to be left out.

It's also important to note that this disciple—whoever he was—said, "Lord, teach us to pray," not, "teach us *a prayer.*" It's not wrong to recite the Lord's Prayer—if nothing else, it helps drive home the point the Lord was making. But He did not prescribe this prayer and these words for the purpose of rote recitation. Instead, what the Lord gives us here is a pattern to follow, a framework onto which we ought to construct our own prayers. He said, "When you pray, say" (11:2)—literally, "When you pray, pray like this." He provided a detailed skeleton to hang all our prayers on. The disciples asked Him how to pray; He's going to show us.

Addressed to Our Father

Christ gives us a model for prayer that begins by addressing God with a familiarity the Jews would have found frighteningly presumptuous. Throughout the Old Testament, God is only occasionally referred to as "Father," but never in the context of a prayer. Christ's frequent use of the term offended and provoked Israel's religious leaders, who rightly understood it as signifying His deity. In response to criticism over His working on the Sabbath, Jesus said, "My Father is working until now, and I Myself am working" (John 5:17). John described the fallout of the confrontation with this postscript: "For this reason therefore the Jews were seeking all the more to kill Him, because He not only was breaking the Sabbath, but also was calling God His own Father, making Himself equal with God" (v. 18).

But Christ did not reserve the use of the term exclusively for Himself. One of the primary points Jesus repeatedly emphasized throughout His public ministry is that God is the Father of all the redeemed. For example, in the Sermon on the Mount, He said, "Your Father knows what you need before you ask Him" (Matt. 6:8). In John 20:17, after His resurrection, Jesus said, "Go to My brethren and say to them, 'I ascend to My Father and your Father.' " Altogether, God is called "Father" sixty-five times in the Synoptic Gospels and another hundred in John's gospel. Christ's arrival signaled the removal of the partition that separated God and man—quite literally, in the aftermath of His crucifixion (Matt. 27:51). Through the Son's sacrificial death, we become children of the Father.

"Father" is translated from the Greek word *patēr*, but the spoken language of the day was Aramaic, so the word Christ likely said was *abba*. This wasn't a formal title. It was an intimate term—usually one of the first words a small child would learn, comparable to "Daddy" or "Papa" today. It's a term that evokes tender affection and familial love. That's how God wants His people to think of Him. "Or what man is there among you who, when his son asks for a loaf, will give him a stone? Or if he asks for a fish, he will not give him a snake, will he? If you then, being evil, know how to give good gifts to your children, how much more will your Father who is in heaven give what is good to those who ask Him!" (Matt. 7:9–11). God wants us to think of Him and refer to Him in this most intimate way. The sovereign, eternal, holy Creator God of the universe wants you and me to call Him Father.

This is an amazing reality. In his epistles, Paul repeatedly emphasizes the familial character of our relationship to the Father. He told the Galatians, "Because you are sons, God has sent forth the Spirit of His Son into our hearts, crying, 'Abba! Father!' " (Gal. 4:6). In Romans 8:15, he wrote, "You have received a spirit of adoption as sons by which we cry out, 'Abba! Father!' " God is not the remote god of the Stoics, unable to feel anything. He is not the god of the Epicureans, living in perfect, indifferent serenity. Neither is He the god of the deists, who wound up the universe and walked away. He is not, as Thomas Hardy wrote in the epic drama *The Dynasts*, "the dreaming, dark, dumb Thing that turns the handle of this idle Show!" He is our Abba Father, the God who intimately knows and loves us.

Consider the story of the prodigal son. The magnanimous affection of the father for his penitent child is overwhelming. The son simply hopes to be a slave in the household, but the father instructs his servants, "Quickly bring out the best robe and put it on him, and put a ring on his hand and sandals on his feet; and bring the fattened calf, kill it, and let us eat and celebrate; for this son of mine was dead and has come to life again; he was lost and has been found" (Luke 15:22–24). The stunning reality is that if you are a redeemed believer, you are that son. That is the lavish, forgiving love the Father has for you, His child forever. His arms are open and He is eager to embrace you.

God is our Father, and that glorious truth is where our prayers begin.

Adoring His Name

While we are rightly thrilled to have unrestricted, immediate access to our heavenly Father—to be able to rush into His presence crying, "Abba! Father!" and spilling out the issues of our hearts to Him—we must also remember that He is sacred and holy. Jesus' instructions for prayer remind us that we must also come soberly and humbly to our Father's offering the honor and respect He is due.

Christ's model for prayer quickly follows the identification of God as our Father with the sobering line "Hallowed be Your name" (Luke 11:2). This is not just a casual bit of religious jargon. It's not a sanctified "Long live the King!" or "God save the Queen!" And we must ensure it doesn't become like that through familiarity. Rather, this is a statement that recognizes the enormous respect required when entering God's holy presence.

The Jews took those cautions to the extreme. They wouldn't say or write the name of God, so they invented other ways to refer to Him without using His name. They treated the name of God as though it was too holy to even speak, and over time their fastidious honor for God's name became a form of legalism.

We don't need to take such an extreme perspective. But in a culture that skews too sentimental and too casual, this is a valuable mandate that our Father's name deserves and demands our respect. As His children, we are welcomed into His presence, but we must be aware that we are walking into the Holy of Holies. While there is familiarity, love, and a personal relationship of affection and generosity, it must be balanced with reverence and awe.

Christ singled out the "name" of God, but the idea is not that we honor that as if it were His *title*. His name is synonymous with His person—all that He is—manifesting itself in all that He does. So the "name" of God is that which refers to the sum of His character, His nature, His attributes, His personality, and His works. In John 17:6, Jesus said, "I have manifested Your name." He meant: "I have manifested You, Your Person, Your power, and Your truth to the men You have given me out of this world. I have put You on display." Honoring the name of God means honoring all that He is and does.

Think about all the additional names of God that identify particular features of the fullness of His holy character. He is called *Elohim*, the name that acknowledges Him as Creator—the third word used in the entire Bible. He is *El-elyon*, "God Most High." In Genesis 14:19, we read, "Blessed be Abram of God Most High, possessor of heaven and earth." He is called *Jehovah-jireh*, "The LORD Will Provide" (Gen. 22:14). He is *Jehovah-nissi*, "The LORD is My Banner" (Ex. 17:15); *Jehovah-ropheka*, "The LORD your healer" (Ex. 15:26); *Jehovah-shalom*, "The LORD is Peace" (Judg. 6:24); *Jehovah-roi*, "The LORD is my shepherd" (Ps. 23:1); *Jehovah-tsidkenu*, "The LORD our righteousness" (Jer. 23:6); *Jehovah-sabaoth*, "The LORD of hosts" (1 Sam. 1:3); *Jehovah-shamah*, "The LORD is there" (Ezek. 48:35), and *Jehovah-meqaddeskem*, "The LORD who sanctifies you" (Ex. 31:13). He is the eternal "I AM" (Ex.

3:14; John 8:58). He's also *Adonai*, "the Lord." His "name" is the sum of all those names and the glorious truths they represent. When we pray, we go to Him as Father, but we must be aware that we are entering the presence of the Lord in His fullness.

The word *hallowed* has become archaic and has mostly dropped out of contemporary use. It is usually associated with cloistered halls, long robes, dismal chants, candles, musty rooms, mournful music, and other high church traditions. However, *hallowed* simply means "to be holy." Swapping out the two brings a little clarity without losing the meaning of Christ's instructions. We address God as *Father* but follow it closely with the reverential reminder *holy be Your name*. This is not a means of bestowing holiness on God's name. Rather, it is clearly recognizing His perfect holiness and honoring Him accordingly. John Calvin said, "For God's Name to be *hallowed* means exactly that God's Name is to be held in the honour which is deserved, that men may never speak or think of Him without the highest reverence."[1] Hallowing God's name is giving voice to our hearts' affirmation that He is to be honored above all things.

This high and exalted view of God is essential as we come to Him in prayer. In one sense, it would be easy to let the words "Hallowed be Your name" thoughtlessly tumble out of our mouths without considering their significance. But such casual blasphemy betrays a heart that is still cold to the truth about God and the glory of His character. Put directly, children of God won't carelessly toss around their Father's name. When we hallow the name of God—that is, when we afford Him the honor He is due—we are affirming that He is set apart from everything common and profane, and that He is to be prized, esteemed, adored, praised, and worshiped as the only One who is infinitely worthy of glory. In his book *The Knowledge of the Holy*, A.W. Tozer wrote, "We must think worthily of God. It is morally imperative that we purge from our minds all ignoble concepts of the Deity and let Him be the God in our minds that He is in His universe."[2]

Hallowing God's name also means we believe He is who He says He is in Scripture. Hebrews 11:6 says, "He who comes to God must believe that He is and that He is a rewarder of those who seek Him." Put simply, we hallow the name of God by faithfully studying His Word to know Him. If we're not truly worshiping the God of the Bible—if we're settling for a deity of our own design, built to suit our whims and interests—then we're only honoring our own imaginations. It is a horrific heresy to redefine God. Hallowing God means knowing and praising Him according to His testimony to Himself in Scripture. If we are to properly honor our Father, we must be passionate, eager students of His truth. We need to echo the words of David in Psalm 16:8: "I have set the LORD continually before me."

We also hallow God's name when we conform our lives to His Word and His will. We can't expect to honor God in prayer if our lives are actively *dishonoring* Him. Churches today are full of men and women who claim the name of Christ but reject Him with their lives and tarnish the testimony of His church. As He warned in the Sermon on the Mount, "Not everyone who says to Me, 'Lord, Lord,' will enter the kingdom of heaven, but he who does the will of My Father who is in heaven will enter" (Matt. 7:21). Our prayer is not just that God's name would be honored in our words but that His name would be magnified and glorified in our thoughts and actions. We desire to live as Christ instructed in Matthew 5:16: "Let your light shine before men in such a way that they may see your good works, and glorify your Father who is in heaven."

Hallowing our Father's name means we can approach Him in confidence and that we do so on our faces, in humble recognition of His holiness.

Advancing the Kingdom

After defining the proper reverential relationship to our Father, Jesus gives us a third instructive phrase in His model prayer: "Your kingdom come" (Luke 11:2). The vain repetition of the Pharisees and the scribes, who sought to somehow badger God into doing what they wanted, is a far cry from what our Lord is telling us here. This emphasis on God's kingdom puts the focus on His sovereignty, which is critical in our prayers. We recognize God as a loving Father, as the source of everything we need. We recognize God as sacred and absolutely holy, and we pursue His glory. And we recognize God as utterly and completely sovereign. Immediately after the celebration of intimacy and the celebration of worship comes submission. "Your

THE CHRISTIAN LIFE MEANS ENGAGING IN PRAYER

kingdom come" is another way for us to say, "Do whatever advances Your kingdom."

The kingdom of God was a central reality in Christ's preaching. Simply put, God's kingdom is the sphere over which He rules. In that sense, there are two kingdoms of God. The first kingdom is His *universal* kingdom: God is the ruler of the entire universe. Revelation 15:3 refers to Him as the "King of the nations." Psalm 103:19 says, "The LORD has established His throne in the heavens, and His sovereignty rules over all." But God's authority over His creation is already absolute—it cannot increase or advance.

Instead, the petition "Your kingdom come" has God's *redemptive* kingdom in view. This speaks to God's sovereign authority over His people, who are His subjects by virtue of salvation. Jesus came preaching the good news of God's kingdom. Throughout His ministry, Christ called sinners to Himself, proclaiming, "Repent, for the kingdom of heaven is at hand" (Matt. 4:17). The King was gathering His people. So in this petition, we are asking the Lord to build His kingdom. We are praying for the advance of the gospel and the salvation of the elect.

As we see from Christ's teaching, there are multiple dimensions to God's redemptive kingdom. In Matthew 8:11, He spoke of its existence in the past, noting the presence of Israel's patriarchs "Abraham, Isaac and Jacob in the kingdom of heaven." He also referred to the kingdom in the present, telling the Jews, "The kingdom of God is in your midst" (Luke 17:21). While commissioning the seventy in Luke 10:9, He instructed them

87

to proclaim, "The kingdom of God has come near to you." But because Israel was looking for a Messiah to institute a political kingdom, they failed to appreciate the arrival of God's spiritual kingdom. Christ also pointed to a future fulfillment of God's kingdom in His Olivet Discourse. Looking ahead to God's judgment and His millennial reign, He said, "Then the King will say to those on His right, 'Come, you who are blessed of My Father, inherit the kingdom prepared for you from the foundation of the world' " (Matt. 25:34). With those dimensions in mind, praying that God's kingdom would come is a shorthand way of saying, "God, do whatever it is that brings the fullness of Your redemptive purposes to fulfillment."

In the parallel instructions found in Matthew 6, Jesus said: "Your kingdom come. Your will be done, on earth as it is in heaven" (Matt. 6:10). What is transpiring in heaven? Heaven is consumed with the exaltation of God, the worship of Christ, and the presence of holiness. It's where God is praised and worshiped by holy saints and angels, and this is a prayer to bring such heavenly features down to earth. The church is to be the place where *heaven comes down*, not the place where *the world comes in*. That is what we pray for: "Lord, bring Your heavenly kingdom down! Build Your kingdom! Exalt Yourself! Exalt Your Son!" Only the true church can be the answer to this prayer.

Notice that no personal requests have yet been made. By now, we should be so lost in wonder, love, and praise that, without even saying so, we gladly yield our temporal concerns and needs to His wisdom and provision. We can't truly pray "Father, hallowed be Your name; Your kingdom come" if we're merely coming to Him to have our needs met. The opening petitions of Christ's model prayer are meant to get our eyes off our plans and fixed on God's glory and His eternal purposes. We're expressing the desire for God to glorify Himself by building His kingdom. We're praying to align with His sovereign will in seeing those whom He chose in eternity past come to Him in salvation.

One might argue, "If God already knows what He is going to do and whom He is going to save, what's the point of praying for it?" While some who take that cavalier perspective believe they are celebrating God's sovereignty, they're actually making a mockery of it. We pray for God's kingdom to come, first and foremost, because He instructed us to. Furthermore, we pray this way because it connects our hearts with God's eternal purposes. Did the Apostle Paul indifferently sit back and assume the elect would eventually come to faith? No, he was a passionate pursuer of the lost, saying, "For I could wish that I myself were accursed, separated from Christ for the sake of my brethren, my kinsmen according to the flesh" (Rom. 9:3). Jesus knows the hearts of men (John 2:25), but He still wept over Jerusalem's unbelief (Matt. 23:37). We should celebrate God's sovereignty without letting it stifle our zeal for intercession or using it as an excuse to refrain from reaching out with the gospel. As Paul wrote in 2 Corinthians 5:11, "Knowing the fear of the Lord, we persuade men."

Ultimately, we pray for God's kingdom to come because we believe the promise of James 5:16—that "the effective prayer of a righteous man can accomplish much." We're not hoping to change God's mind or bend His will to ours. We're praying that He will glorify Himself in the salvation of lost sinners, that He will usher in His eternal kingdom, and that He will use us to do it. Our prayers are a true spiritual means in the accomplishment of His will.

Asking for What We Need

Only after we have properly honored our Father and aligned our hearts to His kingdom purposes do we consider bringing our requests to the Lord in prayer. Christ shows us the framework for our petitions in Luke 11:3–4: "Give us each day our daily bread. And forgive us our sins, for we ourselves also forgive everyone who is indebted to us. And lead us not into temptation." These three short sentences encompass all of man's fundamental needs.

Although our needs are now in focus, God's glory is still the ultimate goal. In fact, each of these requests is tied to a promise from God. Their fulfillment meets our needs, but it also displays the mercy, love, and gracious provision of our heavenly Father. Specifically, in the answers we receive to these requests, we see God function as our supporter, our Savior, and our shelter.

Christ begins with the instruction to ask God, "Give us each day our daily bread" (v. 3). This is not merely a request for food—the term extends to all the essentials of everyday life. It's astounding to think that the immense, transcendent Lord of the universe cares about whether we have enough food or a proper roof over our heads. But that is exactly the point Christ made in the Sermon on the Mount.

> For this reason I say to you, do not be worried about your life, as to what you will eat or what you will drink; nor for your body, as to what you will put on. Is not life more than food, and the body more than clothing? Look at the birds of the air, that they do not sow, nor reap nor gather into barns, and yet your heavenly Father feeds them. Are you not worth much more than they? And who of you by being worried can add a single hour to his life? And why are you worried about clothing? Observe how the lilies of the field grow; they do not toil nor do they spin, yet I say to you that not even Solomon in all his glory clothed himself like one of these. But if God so clothes the grass of the field, which is alive today and tomorrow is thrown into the furnace, will He not much more clothe you? You of little faith! Do not worry then, saying, "What will we eat?" or "What will we drink?" or "What will we wear for clothing?" For the Gentiles eagerly seek all these things; for your heavenly Father knows that you need all these things. But seek first His kingdom and His righteousness, and all these things will be added to you. (Matt. 6:25–33)

With God as our gracious, compassionate supporter, there is no need for worry about how our basic needs will be met. In fact, we should treat such fears as a temptation to doubt both the promises and the goodness and faithfulness of our heavenly Father. When we trust in the Lord to meet our needs, we are trusting in His Word and His inexhaustible resources. Proverbs 10:3 assures us, "The LORD will not allow the righteous to hunger." Paul echoes that promise: "My God will supply all your needs according to His riches in glory in Christ Jesus" (Phil. 4:19).

God's generous supply does not excuse Christians of the duty to work (see 2 Thess. 3:10–12), nor does it guarantee that believers won't face material hardships (see Heb. 11:37). Instead, it means that God, in His sovereign wisdom, will supply us with everything we need to sustain us for our calling in His kingdom.

Christ gives us a second petition to bring to the Lord: "Forgive us our sins" (Luke 11:4). Frankly, our physical needs pale in comparison to this category. Humanity's great need is forgiveness for sin, and that comes through Christ alone. On his own, no person is capable of doing anything to atone for sin and reconcile himself to a holy, righteous God. The prophet Jeremiah vividly illustrated the sinner's spiritual inability: "Can the Ethiopian change his skin or the leopard his spots? Then you also can do good who are accustomed to doing evil" (Jer. 13:23). Paul employed a different metaphor, simply referring to the sinful heart as "dead" (Eph. 2:1). But the glorious news of the gospel is that forgiveness, redemption, and justification are available in our Savior, Jesus Christ. In his epistle to the Colossians, Paul wrote, "When you were dead in your transgressions and the uncircumcision of your flesh, He made you alive together with Him, having forgiven us all our transgressions, having canceled out the certificate of debt consisting of decrees against us, which was hostile to us; and He has taken it out of the way, having nailed it to the cross" (Col. 2:13–14). In the substitutionary sacrifice of Christ, we now stand before God cloaked in the righteousness of His Son. "He made Him who knew no sin to be sin on our behalf, so that we might become the righteousness of God in Him" (2 Cor. 5:21).

As we saw in the previous chapter, believers do not require the full washing of salvation to be repeated every time we sin; we simply need to "wash our feet" (see John 13:10) through faithful, penitent confession. The Apostle John later promised in his first epistle, "If we confess our sins, He is faithful and righteous to forgive us our sins and to cleanse us from all unrighteousness" (1 John 1:9).

Christ includes a prerequisite with this second request to the Lord. We are to ask the Lord to forgive our sins, acknowledging, "For we ourselves also forgive everyone who is indebted to us" (Luke 11:4). Nothing could be more of a blatant contradiction than an unforgiving Christian. Knowing what we have been forgiven in Christ ought to compel us to be gracious and quick to forgive when others sin against us. Rather than cultivating the bitterness and anger that consume this world, we should be grateful for opportunities to dispense the same mercy and forgiveness that our Father has already abundantly poured out on us. That's the point of the Lord's parable in Matthew 18:23–35:

For this reason the kingdom of heaven may be compared to a king who wished to settle accounts with his slaves. When he had begun to settle them, one who owed him ten thousand talents was brought to him. But since he did not have the means to repay, his lord commanded him to be sold, along with his wife and children and all that he had, and repayment to be made. So the slave fell to the ground and prostrated himself before him, saying, "Have patience with me and I will repay you everything." And the lord of that slave felt compassion and released him and forgave him the debt. But that slave went out and found one of his fellow slaves who owed him a hundred denarii; and he seized him and began to choke him, saying, "Pay back what you owe." So his fellow slave fell to the ground and began to plead with him, saying, "Have patience with me and I will repay you." But he was unwilling and went and threw him in prison until he should pay back what was owed. So when his fellow slaves saw what had happened, they were deeply grieved and came and reported to their lord all that had happened. Then summoning him, his lord said to him, "You wicked slave, I forgave you all that debt because you pleaded with me. Should you not also have had mercy on your fellow slave, in the same way that I had mercy on you?" And his lord, moved with anger, handed him over to the torturers until he should repay all that was owed him. My heavenly Father will also do the same

THE CHRISTIAN LIFE MEANS ENGAGING IN PRAYER

to you, if each of you does not forgive his brother from your heart.

Finally, Jesus teaches us to petition our Father for shelter—specifically, for spiritual protection. He closes His model for prayer with the phrase "and lead us not into temptation" (Luke 11:4). This prayer can be confusing at first glance. We know from James that God "does not tempt anyone" (James 1:13). But the concern here is not that God would actually lead us into the snares of the devil.

Rather, this is a means of recognizing the vast array of spiritual threats poised against us and our dependence on the Lord's power and providence to see us through the minefield of this world. It's an echo of David's cry in Psalm 141:8: "My eyes are toward You, O GOD, the Lord; in You I take refuge; do not leave me defenseless." Christ made a similar request on behalf of His disciples: "Keep them from the evil one" (John 17:15).

At the same time, we must acknowledge that the Lord will allow our faith to be tested. In the face of those beneficial trials, we need the steadfast confidence in God's sovereign purposes that Peter described: "In this you greatly rejoice, even though now for a little while, if necessary, you have been distressed by various trials, so that the proof of your faith, being more precious than gold which is perishable, even though tested by fire, may be found to result in praise and glory and honor at the revelation of Jesus Christ" (1 Peter 1:6–7). Praying that temptation won't overtake us in

such trials is effectively asking Him to uphold the promise
He made through the Apostle Paul: "No temptation has
overtaken you but such as is common to man; and God is
faithful, who will not allow you to be tempted beyond
what you are able, but with the temptation will provide the
way of escape also, so that you will be able to endure it"
(1 Cor. 10:13). It's praying for Him to make that way of escape
apparent so that we don't succumb to temptation.

In his *Studies on the Sermon on the Mount,* Dr. Martyn
Lloyd-Jones summed up the significance of these three prayer-
ful petitions:

> Our whole life is found there in those three petitions,
> and that is what makes this prayer so utterly amazing.
> In such a small compass our Lord has covered the whole
> life of the believer in every respect. Our physical needs,
> our mental needs and, of course, our spiritual needs are
> included. The body is remembered, the soul is remem-
> bered, the spirit is remembered. . . . We cannot fail to
> be impressed by the all-inclusiveness of these petitions.
> That does not mean that we should never enter into
> details; we must, we are taught to do so. We are taught
> to bring our life in detail to God in prayer; but here we
> have only the great headings. Our Lord gives us these
> and we fill in the details, but it is important for us to be
> sure that all our petitions should belong under one or
> other of the headings.[3]

Under the guidance of Christ, we come to God as our gracious and loving Father. We hallow His Name. We praise His redemptive work and seek His glory. And we humbly ask Him to meet our needs. As with everything else we do (1 Cor. 10:31), we seek to magnify and glorify our God in the way we commune with Him.

- Chapter Five -

THE CHRISTIAN LIFE MEANS REPUDIATING THE MYTH OF INFLUENCE

A pragmatic myth has been circulating in the church for the last several decades. This myth—let's call it "the myth of influence"—has been proven wrong repeatedly, but its popularity continues to grow virtually unabated. This myth is perhaps the primary cause of the current confusion over the purpose and mission of the church. And in its destructive wake, this myth has left many congregations corrupted and scarred by weak teaching, poor theology, and stifled sanctification.

The myth of influence is that the gospel advances on the backs of public favor and popularity. It's the idea that believers can somehow persuade sinners into the kingdom of God by developing a more attractive message. The myth of influence says that we can attract the lost to the church if we create alliances with the right people, occupy positions of worldly influence, and stylize our churches to reflect consumer trends and thus eliminate consumer resistance. It's the notion that the key to growing the church and winning the lost is a better public relations strategy, a more emotionally engaging worship experience, a stronger social media presence, a more relaxed church environment, an edgier spokesman, a more inclusive worldview, or the enthusiastic embrace of "progressive" social movements.

Our Lord clearly revealed that the sinner's resistance to God's Word is the natural response of all fallen humanity. It is universal, profound, and it cannot be altered or mitigated by human strategy. Hear the Lord's diagnosis in John 8:42–47:

> If God were your Father, you would love Me, for I proceeded forth and have come from God, for I have not even come on My own initiative, but He sent Me. Why do you not understand what I am saying? It is because you cannot hear My word. You are of your father the devil, and you want to do the desires of your father. He was a murderer from the beginning, and does not stand in the truth because there is no truth in him. Whenever he speaks a lie, he speaks from his own nature, for he is a liar and the father of lies. But because I speak the truth, you do not believe Me. Which one of you convicts Me of sin? If I speak truth, why do you not believe Me? He who is of God hears the words of God; for this reason you do not hear them, because you are not of God.

REPUDIATING THE MYTH OF INFLUENCE

Make no mistake—any effort to overcome this condition by human means is a deeply flawed scheme, and a myriad of compromises are made in the process. The pursuit of cultural influence inevitably leads to the development of a nonthreatening message of inclusive salvation that seeks to eliminate all offenses. It attempts to make the church look, sound, and feel like a big Starbucks; it emphasizes comfort and pop culture appeal with the hope that we might subtly lure people into the kingdom.

Those strategies are impotent and futile. Scripture reveals that there is only one way into the kingdom, and it is through the gate of the pure gospel alone. The cruel irony is that even when churches pursue all kinds of clever marketing tactics, people will only enter the kingdom when they understand and believe the true gospel—the word of the cross, as revealed in Scripture. The gospel does not advance on the back of public favor; it advances only by the Holy Spirit's work through the Word of God, *in the face of and in spite of public hostility.*

In its most superficial form, the myth of influence reasons, "If they think we're cool, they'll think Jesus is cool too." Serious worship disappears along with the public ordinances. Theological exposition of Scripture vanishes. Transcendence and profundity are exchanged for mimicking shallow, worldly, adolescent styles. Church discipline disappears, holiness is minimalized, and sin is normalized. Despite all those exchanges, the myth maintains that these methods will usher people into the kingdom.

To be clear, I want to help lead people into the kingdom. I understand what was in the heart of John Knox when he pleaded with the Lord, "Give me Scotland, or I die." I want to see the lost redeemed and the slaves of sin set free. I want to see society changed and righteousness prevail. But the only way it can be changed is through the power of the Spirit and the truth of the gospel. There is no other hope for the spiritually dead, no other means by which the Holy Spirit makes dead sinners alive in Christ. We have to center our evangelistic efforts on the pure, unadulterated gospel of Jesus Christ, or those evangelistic efforts are in vain.

And despite the efforts of some to accessorize with fashion and culture and sugarcoat the gospel, it cannot be made attractive to the eyes of the unbeliever. In the eyes of the unsaved, the gospel will always be offensive, shameful, scandalous, and hard to believe. That is how the Lord intended it, as He clearly stated in Luke 14:26–27: "If anyone comes to Me, and does not hate his own father and mother and wife and children and brothers and sisters, yes, and even his own life, he cannot be My disciple. Whoever does not carry his own cross and come after Me cannot be My disciple."

The Shameful Gospel

The gospel produces hostility. It is popular to attempt to alter it, not only to make it easier for people to believe but to take some of the heat off themselves for presenting it. In fact, the word of the cross is so shameful and antagonizing that even faithful Christians struggle to proclaim the true gospel, afraid of the rejection, ridicule, and embarrassment it will bring. That's why it is hard for even some Christian leaders, when they get on television in secular settings, to speak the gospel with honesty and clarity. Sometimes they can't even seem to get the name "Jesus" out of their mouths.

Paul warned Timothy against such fearful timidity, urging his apprentice in the faith, "Do not be ashamed of the testimony of our Lord" (2 Tim. 1:8). He included a similar exhortation against spiritual cowardice in Romans 1:16, saying, "For I am not ashamed of the gospel, for it is the power of God for salvation to everyone who believes." At first, these seem like bizarre statements. Why would a preacher—or an *Apostle*, for that matter—be ashamed of the gospel? A scientist or a doctor wouldn't need to overcome his shame to announce he had found the cure for cancer. Why is it, then, that even popular preachers struggle to speak boldly when proclaiming the Lord Jesus as the only cure for sin and its dread consequences? What is the source of this shame that silences God's people and compels them to dull the sharp edges of the gospel? Why the search for an inoffensive abridgment of God's plan to save sinners?

Put simply, to believe the gospel goes against everything that is natural in man. In Paul's first epistle to the Corinthians, we read:

> For the word of the cross is foolishness to those who are perishing, but to us who are being saved it is the power of God. For it is written, "I will destroy the wisdom of the wise, and the cleverness of the clever I will set aside." Where is the wise man? Where is the scribe? Where is

the debater of this age? Has not God made foolish the wisdom of the world? For since in the wisdom of God the world through its wisdom did not come to know God, God was well-pleased through the foolishness of the message preached to save those who believe. (1:18–21)

All the religious alliances, the positions of power and influence, the posturing to leverage the trends and interests of the world—none of it can make the gospel any more attractive or acceptable to children of Satan. By God's design, the cross of Christ *is* offensive. And rather than trying to apologize for it or soften its shameful nature, we need to be faithful to simply proclaim it. We need to love sinners enough to offend them with the truth.

The Horror of the Cross

In 1 Corinthians 1, Paul highlights several of the facets of the gospel that make its message offensive and shameful to the world. Picking up where we left off in verses 22 and 23, he points to the *shameful stigma* of the cross. He writes, "For indeed Jews ask for signs and Greeks search for wisdom; but we preach Christ crucified, to Jews a stumbling block and to Gentiles foolishness." "Foolishness" is *moria* in the Greek—it's the word from which we get the term *moron*. The word of the cross is moronic to those who are unregenerate. It is idiotic. Specifically, the idea of God dying on a cross was ridiculous, both to the Jews and the gentiles.

According to verse 22, the Jews sought a sign—some kind of heavenly supernatural evidence that indicated that the true Messiah had come. Instead, God gave them a stumbling block. To Israel, a crucified Messiah was bizarre, offensive, and blasphemous. The Greeks, on the other hand, sought wisdom. They wanted some transcendental, elevated, esoteric knowledge. They saw the idea that the eternal Creator of the universe would hang on a cross as utter stupidity.

A little background is helpful to our understanding why the Jews and gentiles viewed the cross with such loathing. Crucifixion was a systematized series of events including flogging, carrying the cross beam, wearing a condemning sign over one's neck, and then being tied or nailed to the crossbar, hoisted to an upright post, and left there suspended, stark naked before the view of everyone. Death could be hurried by shattering the legs, but this slight mercy was usually not afforded, so that victims could suffer for days. The final indignity was leaving the naked corpse exposed in the sun to become carrion for birds.

Crucifixion was considered such a severe indignity and an extreme punishment that Rome did not inflict it on its own citizens, except in the case of treason. For the most part, it was reserved for conquered enemies, notorious criminals, and rebellious slaves. The Roman Empire's policies on crucifixion led Romans to view the crucified with contempt and disgust. It was the kind of death that those in polite society didn't discuss. And although it was an obscene and shameful way to die, it was relatively common, making Christ's murder horrifying but also somewhat unremarkable. In the eyes of the unbelieving world, this was certainly not a death befitting a divine king.

The Jewish antipathy toward crucifixion was all of that and more. They detested the Roman practice, holding it in higher contempt than the pagans did. But they went beyond that. They saw a crucified person as one who bore the curse of God, as Deuteronomy 21:23 states, "For he who is hanged is accursed of God." Dying a common death, the kind reserved for the most wretched criminals, and bearing the curse of God was not what the Jews would have ever expected from the Messiah. The claim was scandalous. The Jews did not crucify people, but history tells us they did hang up dead bodies—particularly blasphemers and idolaters. After they were stoned, some were put up on a cross to fulfill Deuteronomy 21:23, a visible reminder that they were cursed by God.

These pervasive attitudes toward crucifixion posed a massive obstacle to the gospel in the first century. When we think of a cross, we think of something pretty and ornate that hangs in our churches or around our necks. But to the Jews and gentiles of the day, it was scurrilous and scandalous, a stumbling block of foolishness, and idiocy. There was no way to make that message acceptable in the first-century world. To Jew or gentile, it would have been hard to believe that the Son of God incarnate, the Messiah, suffered and died like the lowest of criminals. Yet the gospel actually called the Jews to believe in as Savior and surrender to the very One they considered a blasphemer, "smitten of God, and afflicted" (Isa. 53:4). Humanly speaking, God could not have put a more formidable barrier to repentance and faith in their way.

The good news of the cross appeared to be an absurdity and an obscenity, and it remains so to this day. Looking at the cross—even from the safe distance of two thousand years—we are still rightly repulsed by the horror of Christ's death. And to the mind that has not been illuminated by the Spirit, there is an apparent disconnect between who Jesus said He was and how He died. The humility and shame of the Lord's death is too much for the unrepentant mind to comprehend. The reality of that death being a substitutionary sacrifice for guilty sinners, who must repent and believe or be condemned to hell forever, was, and remains, the least seeker-friendly message imaginable.

The Futility of the Mind

The offense of the gospel isn't limited to the cross. Paul also identifies its *shameful simplicity*. Returning to 1 Corinthians 1:19–21, the Apostle writes:

> For it is written, "I will destroy the wisdom of the wise, and the cleverness of the clever I will set aside." Where is the wise man? Where is the scribe? Where is the debater of this age? Has not God made foolish the wisdom of the world? For since in the wisdom of God the world through its wisdom did not come to know God, God was well-pleased through the foolishness of the message preached to save those who believe.

Both Jews and gentiles were into complexity. The Jews found theirs mostly in the rabbinical traditions. But the gentiles—the Greeks, in particular—loved exploring philosophy, metaphysics, mental gymnastics, and intellectual labyrinths. They believed that the truth is knowable only to those who have exalted knowledge and elevated insights. They were awash in philosophies and schools of thought vying for supremacy. The pursuit of intellectual complexities and transcendental knowledge was woven throughout their thinking.

The gospel has no sensitivity to that. It leaves no room for Gnosticism, and it pays no homage to the human mind. It has no interest in complex, esoteric insight. God says He will destroy the wisdom of the wise and the cleverness of the clever, followed by these mocking statements: "Where is the wise man? Where is the scribe? Where is the debater of this age?" (v. 20). This is a comprehensive denunciation of all the accumulated insight, understanding, and wisdom of the world's elite minds. They have nothing to offer when it comes to true, spiritual knowledge of God and His truth. In that sense, the gospel effectively attacks the wisdom of the world. Human insight and intuition are fickle and unreliable. The sinful mind has no capacity to reason its way to God or His kingdom. The truth God has revealed for salvation is beyond the natural mind of man: "But a natural man does not accept the things of the Spirit of God, for they are foolishness to him; and he cannot understand them, because they are spiritually appraised" (1 Cor. 2:14).

God planned it this way. He ordained that no one could come to know Him through human wisdom. The prophet

Jeremiah said, "The wise men are put to shame, they are dismayed and caught; behold, they have rejected the word of the LORD, and what kind of wisdom do they have?" (Jer. 8:9). So, the gospel is also offensive because it collides with the sinner's intellectual, moral, and religious pride.

The Lack of Options

Paul points us to a third offensive aspect of the gospel—we'll call it the *shameful singularity*. In 1 Corinthians 1:23, he simply asserts, "We preach Christ crucified." There are no other options, no alternative means of entrance into God's kingdom. The message of the gospel is straightforward and exclusive. Christ Himself said, "I am the way, and the truth, and the life; no one comes to the Father but through Me" (John 14:6). The Bible resounds with the testimony that "there is salvation in no one else; for there is no other name under heaven that has been given among men by which we must be saved" (Acts 4:12).

But in these postmodern times, that is far too narrow to believe. Even some in the evangelical church would argue that sinners can be saved without the gospel, without the Bible, and without ever knowing who the true God is or ever hearing the name of Jesus. They understand that an exclusive gospel is the only thing this culture of tolerance cannot tolerate. So they devise an accommodating false gospel and a wideness in God's grace that have no basis in Scripture.[1] They preach that God loves everyone just the way they are (giving them permission to *stay the way they are*). They deceptively offer false affection from God, who hates sin and is "angry with the wicked every day" (Ps. 7:11, NKJV; see Ps. 2:12). In fact, there's no discussion of sin and its consequences, no thought to the threat of hell or even a potential eternity in heaven. The focus of the postmodern gospel is almost exclusively on the sinner's felt needs, unfulfilled dreams, and victim status. It reduces Christ to a cosmic life coach whose primary focus is helping us get the maximum satisfaction out of this life.

That simply isn't the gospel. In Luke 9:23, Christ said, "If anyone wishes to come after Me, he must deny himself, and take up his cross daily and follow Me." This is the gospel of self-denial, not self-fulfillment. True faith in Christ is not about becoming all that we can be in this life. Rather, coming to God's kingdom means coming to the end of ourselves. It's the attitude reflected in the repentant cries of the tax collector in Christ's parable. Contrasting the arrogant hypocrisy of Israel's religious leaders, Jesus said, "But the tax collector, standing some distance away, was even unwilling to lift up his eyes to heaven, but was beating his breast, saying, 'God, be merciful to me, the sinner!' " (Luke 18:13). Like the tax collector, we come to Christ only when we understand there is no other hope for us. We turn to the cross because we understand the vast array of human religions are all based on the same lie—that good works can merit the favor of God. Until the vain idol of self-righteousness is finally shattered in our hearts, we cannot come to true faith and repentance. We can't enter the kingdom of God while holding on to the false notion that we in any way earned our acceptance with God. The sinner's only hope for salvation is to recognize his condition and its damning consequences and flee to Christ alone.

In Matthew 13:44, Jesus says, "The kingdom of heaven is like a treasure hidden in the field, which a man found and hid again; and from joy over it he goes and sells all that he has and buys that field." The gospel is offensive because sinners refuse to believe there is only one treasure buried in the field, and they have to "sell all" they have to receive it.

The Disputed Verdict

The gospel is also offensive to the world from the perspective of its *shameful sentence*. In 1 Corinthians 1:18, Paul writes, "For the word of the cross is foolishness to those who are perishing." The phrase "those who are perishing" refers to those who are ruined, destroyed, and on their way to hell. The cross is shameful in the eyes of the world because of the dire sentence it reveals—that the sinner is hopelessly headed for eternal judgment.

Christ was crucified to rescue sinners from God's eternal wrath, so as we proclaim the gospel, we must address that reality at the very outset. The formidable foundation of all gospel presentation must be an inescapable indictment of the eternally damning guilt for constant crimes against God that rests on every human being. Those who seek to make the gospel palatable and popular will always ignore or soften these truths significantly, if not eliminate them altogether. Nothing is more offensive for the sinner to accept than the fact that he is under such a severe condemnation.

A stunning story from the life of our Lord illustrates that point. At the beginning of Christ's ministry in Galilee, He returned to the synagogue in His hometown of Nazareth and delivered a provocative and convicting message to those in attendance. Luke's gospel records the incident:

And the book of the prophet Isaiah was handed to Him. And He opened the book and found the place where it was written, "The Spirit of the Lord is upon Me, because He anointed Me to preach the gospel to the poor. He has sent Me to proclaim release to the captives, and recovery of sight to the blind, to set free those who are oppressed, to proclaim the favorable year of the Lord." And He closed the book, gave it back to the attendant and sat down; and the eyes of all in the synagogue were fixed on Him. And He began to say to them, "Today this Scripture has been fulfilled in your hearing." (4:17–21)

The passage Jesus read was a messianic prophecy from Isaiah 61, and those in the audience would have recognized it as such. His affirmation that "today this Scripture has been fulfilled in your hearing" was an unmistakable claim that He was the long-awaited Messiah. Luke records that the reaction was mixed: "All were speaking well of Him," but also some "were saying, 'Is this not Joseph's son?' " (Luke 4:22). It would have been difficult for them to believe that the young man they watched grow up was actually the Son of God and their Savior.

Acknowledging their doubt, Jesus said, "No doubt you will quote this proverb to Me, 'Physician, heal yourself! Whatever we heard was done at Capernaum, do here in your hometown as well' " (v. 23). He knew they wanted Him to verify His claim with the same signs and wonders they'd heard about from neighboring communities. But no one ever rejected Christ because of a lack of evidence. John 12:37 says, "But though He had performed so many signs before them, yet they were not believing in Him." Knowing the inevitability of their unbelief, the Lord said, "Truly I say to you, no prophet is welcome in his hometown" (Luke 4:24).

And to further prove His point, Jesus reminded them of two prophets who were famously unwelcome. "But I say to you in truth, there were many widows in Israel in the days of Elijah, when the sky was shut up for three years and six months, when a great famine came over all the land; and yet Elijah was sent to none of them, but only to Zarephath, in the land of Sidon, to a woman who was a widow. And there were many lepers in Israel in the time of Elisha the prophet; and none of them was cleansed, but only Naaman the Syrian" (vv. 25–27). Both of those incidents would have been deeply offensive to the Jews.

In each case, Jesus pointed out that God blessed people the Israelites would have considered rejected enemies. The widow in Zarephath, although a God-fearing gentile, lived in a nation dominated by idol worship that was also the homeland of Jezebel. The tale was particularly galling because the drought and ensuing famine had been a divine judgment on Israel's apostasy, and the aid God sent this gentile woman He denied to His covenant people. In the same way, God showed mercy to Naaman, the pagan leader of an opposing military force who lived a blasphemous, immoral life before he humbled himself and obeyed the Lord.

Christ's point was clear. If Israel did not recognize their spiritual condition—if they refused to admit that they were poor, prisoners, blind, and oppressed—God would not bestow His grace and favor on them. Jesus was telling them that the gospel comes to those who know they are spiritually bankrupt, prisoners to their sin, and under judgment. Israel was blind to those realities, and they bore an immense, intolerable weight of guilt, carrying them to eternal punishment.

The Jews sitting in the synagogue that day were offended by such an indictment because they saw themselves not as spiritually poor but as spiritually rich. They were the devout, faithful members of the synagogue. They kept the ceremonies and the Sabbath. They believed they had achieved a certain status by their devotion to the law and to ceremony. In short, they were utterly self-righteous. And they reacted in much the same way sinners do today to the charges and the eternal condemnation against them. "And all the people in the synagogue were filled with rage as they heard these things; and they got up and drove Him out of the city, and led Him to the brow of the hill on which their city had been built, in order to throw Him down the cliff. But passing through their midst, He went His way" (vv. 28–30).

Sinners don't naturally tolerate the confrontation of their sin or the reality of the judgment and wrath it demands. Out of self-love and self-preservation, they will do everything they can to shout down and silence the truth about their desperate situation and need for the Savior. But we cannot acquiesce to that natural hostility. God's people must hold fast to the truth about sin and its dread consequences. We must be faithful to prosecute sinners for the guilt of their offenses against God. Every gospel presentation must begin with a clear and thorough explanation of what they need to be saved *from*.

The Unremarkable Evangelists

It's not merely the facts of Christ's death and the theological realities of the gospel that the world finds offensive. As Paul explains, sinners are just as likely to be offended by the messengers of God's truth—what we'll call the *shameful society*. He writes,

> For consider your calling, brethren, that there were not many wise according to the flesh, not many mighty, not many noble; but God has chosen the foolish things of the world to shame the wise, and God has chosen the weak things of the world to shame the things which are strong, and the base things of the world and the despised God has chosen, the things that are not, so that He may nullify the things that are. (1 Cor. 1:26–28)

Not only do we have a message that is hard to believe, but we also have a message that is delivered by people the world finds hard to respect. The Lord didn't put His gospel into the hands of the most famous, the most notable, or even the most well spoken. He didn't leverage social influencers or pop culture icons to proclaim His truth. He chose *us*. And that lack of star power and name recognition can be offensive to the world.

Paul delineates just how unimpressive God's people are in the world's eyes. He says there are "not many wise, not many mighty, not many noble"—that is, not many intellectuals, not many who wield power and influence, and not many highborn aristocrats. Rather, God has chosen the foolish, weak, base, and despised things of the world. The Lord is pleased to use the nonintellectuals, the unimpressive and insignificant, the unremarkable, and the forgettable to spread His truth. Paul even says He chose "the things that are not"—literally, *the nobodies*.

Why wouldn't God use famous people as His spokesmen? Why wouldn't He employ royals and monarchs, political heavyweights, or the most popular talking heads and tastemakers to promote His gospel? Paul tells us in verse 29: "So that no man may boast before God." Salvation isn't accomplished through the force of personality, and the gospel isn't made more powerful by clever words or a silver tongue. God specifically chose His unremarkable evangelists so that they would never be the explanation for the work of the gospel. He doesn't want His people to get confused about who is performing the transforming work of salvation in sinners' lives.

Paul reinforces that point in his second epistle to the Corinthians. He writes: "For we do not preach ourselves but Christ Jesus as Lord, and ourselves as your bond-servants for Jesus' sake. For God, who said, 'Light shall shine out of darkness,' is the One who has shone in our hearts to give the Light of the knowledge of the glory of God in the face of Christ. But we have this treasure in earthen vessels, so that the surpassing greatness of the power will be of God and not from ourselves" (2 Cor. 4:5–7).

Again, we see that God wants to glorify Himself. There will never be a human explanation for any effective advance of the gospel. There *cannot* be a human explanation because we are nothing but "earthen vessels." Clay pots were cheap, unrefined, breakable, ugly, replaceable, and valueless. We are clay pots. The glory of the gospel is indicated in verse 6 as light shining out of darkness—the light of God shining in the face of Jesus Christ. And we carry this gospel revelation to the world. God has determined to put the glorious message of salvation in a dingy, nondescript pot.

That idea is extended in 2 Timothy 2:20 where Paul says, "In a large house there are not only gold and silver vessels, but also vessels of wood and of earthenware, and some to honor and some to dishonor." Gold and silver vessels were those on which food was served—they're the honorable vessels. On the other hand, clay pots were used to dispose of garbage and excrement. The Apostle Paul is essentially saying, "We have the glory of God in a privy pot." Paul understood that messengers of the gospel must never overestimate their importance.

From the founding of the church, it was never God's plan to leverage worldly influence for the work of the gospel. The early preachers of the gospel were not the elite intellectuals of Egypt, Greece, Rome, or even Israel. The greatest scholars of the day were in Egypt, the most distinguished philosophers were in Athens, the powerful were in Rome, and the biblical scholars were in Jerusalem. By comparison, the disciples were painfully ordinary men. Not one was a priest; not one was a scribe; not one was a ruler of a synagogue. Not one was a Pharisee, and none of them had any educational credentials or occupied a position of influence. Up to seven of them may have been fishermen who made their living with their hands. One was a terrorist; another was a tax collector. From the world's perspective, it was not an impressive group.

But for the true servant of God, the esteem of the world is unimportant. Paul's priority was preaching Christ, and the progress of His kingdom depended on the Holy Spirit's implanting the gospel in hearts.

> We are fools for Christ's sake, but you are prudent in Christ; we are weak, but you are strong; you are distinguished, but we are without honor. To this present hour we are both hungry and thirsty, and are poorly clothed, and are roughly treated, and are homeless; and we toil, working with our own hands; when we are reviled, we bless; when we are persecuted, we endure; when we are slandered, we try to conciliate; we have become as the scum of the world, the dregs of all things, even until now. (1 Cor. 4:10–13)

It is a wonder of God's sovereignty that He uses those that the world views as the scum and the dregs to deliver His gospel of grace. And we can preach His truth with confidence, knowing that no one's salvation depends on us. We cannot empower anyone to new life. We are just the clay pots who enjoy the immense privilege of a high calling in the household of God.

The Humbling Truth

Finally, Paul identifies one last source of offense that the world cannot tolerate—the *shameful sovereignty* of the gospel. In 1 Corinthians 1:30, he writes, "By His doing you are in Christ Jesus, who became to us wisdom from God, and righteousness and sanctification, and redemption." There's no room in God's plan of salvation for man's effort or merit. It's not about a decision the sinner makes or a change he initiates. Paul says God's people are saved "by His doing" alone.

The Lord's sovereign work of salvation is on display throughout His Word. Paul puts it succinctly in his second letter to the Thessalonians when he writes, "God has chosen you from the beginning for salvation through sanctification by the Spirit and faith in the truth" (2 Thess. 2:13). He expands on the same reality in his epistle to the Ephesians.

Blessed be the God and Father of our Lord Jesus Christ, who has blessed us with every spiritual blessing in the heavenly places in Christ, just as He chose us in Him before the foundation of the world, that we would be holy and blameless before Him. In love He predestined us to adoption as sons through Jesus Christ to Himself, according to the kind intention of His will, to the praise of the glory of His grace, which He freely bestowed on us in the Beloved. (Eph. 1:3–6)

But the heart bent by sin and rebellion cannot tolerate a sovereign Savior. Sinners can't stomach the idea that "our God is in the heavens; He does whatever He pleases" (Ps. 115:3). Their false sense of autonomy demands that they have some say in their eternal destiny and that they get some of the credit for "inviting Christ into their lives." That's why it's so easy for people to reject the fundamental truth of the gospel—that "man is not justified by the works of the Law but through faith in Christ Jesus" (Gal. 2:16)—and choose a false religion of works-righteousness, one that soothes their burning consciences by stroking their egos.

Ultimately, the unrepentant heart will not accept what the Bible says about its lost condition. Sinners refuse to believe that they are truly "dead in [their] trespasses and sins" (Eph. 2:1). They want to believe there is still some life in the wretched corpse, that they still possess the means to reach out to God whenever they decide to. More than that, they want God to grade all mankind on a curve. Sinners excel at favorably comparing themselves to one another—they can always find a worse, more egregious example to point to, as though the

righteous and holy Judge was moved by excuses and exe
tions. And when they finally realize that they can't plead d
their sentence, they make a vain attempt for a mistrial
questioning God's right to judge them in the first place. T
Apostle Paul has an answer for that rebellious gripe too: "WI
are you, O man, who answers back to God? The thing molde
will not say to the molder, 'Why did you make me like this,
will it?" (Rom. 9:20).

The tragedy is that the eyes blinded by sin cannot see
the all-sufficient grace and mercy in God's sovereign work of
salvation.

> But God, being rich in mercy, because of His great love
> with which He loved us, even when we were dead in
> our transgressions, made us alive together with Christ
> (by grace you have been saved), and raised us up with
> Him, and seated us with Him in the heavenly places
> in Christ Jesus, so that in the ages to come He might
> show the surpassing riches of His grace in kindness
> toward us in Christ Jesus. For by grace you have been
> saved through faith; and that not of yourselves, it is the
> gift of God; not as a result of works, so that no one may
> boast. For we are His workmanship, created in Christ
> Jesus for good works, which God prepared beforehand
> so that we would walk in them. (Eph. 2:4–10)

The only hope for any sinner is the pride-slaughtering, par-
adoxical shame of the gospel. He must embrace the *shameful*

stigma of the cross and the ignoble horrors of Christ's death on his behalf. He must accept the *shameful simplicity* of the gospel and his inability to reason his way into heaven. He must acknowledge the *shameful singularity* of the gospel—that there are no other options for the salvation of his soul. He must agree with the gospel's *shameful sentence*, acknowledging the dire consequences of his sin. He must embrace the *shameful society* of the gospel, that they are the lowly and those whom society does not respect. And he must submit to the *shameful sovereignty* of the gospel, surrendering his self-righteous works and clinging to the Lord Jesus for justification by grace alone through faith alone in Him alone.

Why are sinners irrevocably offended by the gospel? Why aren't the church's attempts to accommodate and curry favor with the world leading more people into God's kingdom? How do we know the myth of influence is really a myth?

Paul's testimony to his own gospel ministry gives us the answer:

> When I came to you, brethren, I did not come with superiority of speech or of wisdom, proclaiming to you the testimony of God. For I determined to know nothing among you except Jesus Christ, and Him crucified. I was with you in weakness and in fear and in much trembling, and my message and my preaching were not in persuasive words of wisdom, but in demonstration of the Spirit and of power, so that your faith would not rest on the wisdom of men, but on the power of God. (1 Cor. 2:1–5)

If we truly want to be instruments God uses to bring sinners to salvation, we must follow the Word of God and pray for the Spirit of God to give repentance, faith, and eternal blessing to those who hear the truth.

- Chapter Six -

THE CHRISTIAN LIFE MEANS PERSEVERING TO THE END

The year was 1643. The place was Westminster Abbey's Jerusalem Chamber. The greatest theological minds and biblical scholars in England—the Puritans—gathered with lords and commissioners from Parliament for five years of intense study and discussion. Their goal was to institute new reforms to the Church of England and produce a statement of doctrine true to the Scripture and faithful to the gospel. By June 1648, they had completed and ratified the Westminster Confession of Faith. That influential creed contains a brief and unambiguous statement on the eternal security of salvation, a doctrine it refers to simply as "perseverance." In chapter 17, section 1, the Westminster Confession says, "They, whom God hath accepted in his Beloved, effectually called, and sanctified by his Spirit, can neither totally nor finally fall away from the state of grace, but shall certainly persevere therein to the end, and be eternally saved."

Scripture is full of promises that led to this creed and conviction. The Bible is clear on the perseverance of the saints—the promise that those who are truly saved will be brought into eternal glory. "My sheep," Christ said, "hear My voice, and I know them, and they follow Me; and I give eternal life to them, and they will never perish; and no one will snatch them out of My hand. My Father, who has given them to Me, is greater than all; and no one is able to snatch them out of the Father's hand" (John 10:27–29). Whomever God gives to the Son as part of the Son's bride (the church) will be there at the wedding feast in glory. The Lord promises:

All that the Father gives Me will come to Me, and the one who comes to Me I will certainly not cast out. For I have come down from heaven, not to do My own will, but the will of Him who sent Me. This is the will of Him who sent Me, that of all that He has given Me I lose nothing, but raise it up on the last day. For this is the will of My Father, that everyone who beholds the Son and believes in Him will have eternal life, and I Myself will raise him up on the last day. (John 6:37–40; see John 17:6, 9, 12)

In 1 Corinthians 1:7–9, Paul affirms this glorious truth: "You are not lacking in any gift, awaiting eagerly the revelation of our Lord Jesus Christ, who will also confirm you to the end, blameless in the day of our Lord Jesus Christ. God is faithful, through whom you were called into fellowship with His Son,

Jesus Christ our Lord." He gave a similar guarantee to the Thessalonians: "Now may the God of peace Himself sanctify you entirely; and may your spirit and soul and body be preserved complete, without blame at the coming of our Lord Jesus Christ. Faithful is He who calls you, and He also will bring it to pass" (1 Thess. 5:23–24). That is the promise of God to His redeemed. Another beloved benediction at the end of Jude says, "Now to Him who is able to keep you from stumbling, and to make you stand in the presence of His glory blameless with great joy, to the only God our Savior, through Jesus Christ our Lord, be glory, majesty, dominion and authority, before all time and now and forever. Amen" (Jude 24–25).

Perseverance, Not Perfection

Scripture promises us that eternal life is actually *eternal*. That revelation was widely understood by the Westminster divines, but they also understood what perseverance does not mean. It does not mean that Christians never fail in their lives in the area of obedience. It does not mean that those failures won't be serious. Among the Corinthians, Paul noted that many were weak and sick, and some had even died for how they abused the Lord's Table (1 Cor. 11:29–30). For that reason, the Westminster Confession also states,

> Nevertheless, they may, through the temptations of Satan and of the world, the prevalency of corruption remaining in them, and the neglect of their means of

their preservation, fall into grievous sins; and, for a time, continue therein: whereby they incur God's displeasure, and grieve his Holy Spirit, come to be deprived of some measure of their graces and comforts, have their hearts hardened, and their consciences wounded; hurt and scandalize others, and bring temporal judgments upon themselves. (WCF 17.3)

In other words, the divines understood that perseverance in the faith does not mean perfection. Even though believers may sin seriously and repeatedly, there are some things they will never abandon. They will not surrender to the full dominion of sin. They will not lose confidence in the Lord and the gospel. They will not shun holiness and fully embrace iniquity.

And when someone who had professed faith later abandons the gospel, that's not a failure of eternal life. Rather, it's evidence of a superficial faith. As John wrote in his first epistle, "They went out from us, but they were not really of us; for if they had been of us, they would have remained with us; but they went out, so that it would be shown that they all are not of us" (1 John 2:19). Apostasy from the gospel is proof that true faith was never present to begin with—if they had believed, they would have remained. Because they departed, we can say with confidence that they never believed in the first place.

If it were possible for believers to lose salvation, we certainly would. Those who believe it is possible to forfeit eternity are predicating the security of their salvation on their own spiritual strength and self-discipline—which indicates that they have a warped view of the weakness of man's flesh and his will. They misunderstand the words of Christ, who said, "The one who endures to the end, he will be saved" (Matt. 24:13). If it were up to us to hold fast to the faith in our own strength, we would have no hope of heaven. We don't keep ourselves in the faith. Instead, we are secure because we possess a persevering faith that belongs to eternal life.

The doctrine of perseverance teaches that the life that is from God is permanent. Many texts of Scripture teach this concept. For our purposes, we'll focus on 1 Peter 1:3–9:

Blessed be the God and Father of our Lord Jesus Christ, who according to His great mercy has caused us to be born again to a living hope through the resurrection of Jesus Christ from the dead, to obtain an inheritance which is imperishable and undefiled and will not fade away, reserved in heaven for you, who are protected by the power of God through faith for a salvation ready to be revealed in the last time. In this you greatly rejoice, even though now for a little while, if necessary, you have been distressed by various trials, so that the proof of your faith, being more precious than gold which is perishable, even though tested by fire, may be found to result in praise and glory and honor at the revelation of Jesus Christ; and though you have not seen Him, you love Him, and though you do not see Him now, but believe in Him, you greatly rejoice with joy

inexpressible and full of glory, obtaining as the outcome of your faith the salvation of your souls.

Speaking from Personal Experience

Peter was a fitting choice to receive revelation about perseverance. According to Scripture, none of our Lord's disciples
(other than the apostate Judas) stumbled more consistently or
more miserably than Peter, at least as far as the Gospels record.
If ever there was one prone to spiritual failure, it was him.

Consider the speed with which Peter would alternate
between profound and profoundly stupid. In Matthew 16:16,
Peter said, "You are the Christ, the Son of the living God." The
Lord commended him for such spiritual insight, saying, "Flesh
and blood did not reveal this to you, but My Father who is in
heaven" (v. 17). From that point, Matthew tells us that Christ
began to speak more explicitly about what He was soon to suffer (v. 21). And in no time at all, Scripture tells us, "Peter took
Him aside and began to rebuke Him, saying, 'God forbid it,
Lord! This shall never happen to You.' But He turned and said
to Peter, 'Get behind Me, Satan! You are a stumbling block to
Me; for you are not setting your mind on God's interests, but
man's' " (vv. 22–23).

Peter is proof that a true believer can stumble but not
fall. Jesus had said to him, "Simon, Simon, behold, Satan has
demanded permission to sift you like wheat; but I have prayed
for you, that your faith may not fail" (Luke 22:31–32). Christ's
intercessory prayer for the preservation of Peter's faith would

be answered, but not through Peter's own strength and ability. However, the impetuous disciple's response demonstrates that Peter believed he had the power to hold on. He said, "Lord, with You I am ready to go both to prison and to death!" (v. 33). Peter's confidence in himself was woefully misplaced, and the Lord was about to show him. He replied, "I say to you, Peter, the rooster will not crow today until you have denied three times that you know Me" (v. 34). Despite his good intentions, Peter's flesh would fail within hours. But his faith would not fail, because Jesus was interceding on his behalf to sustain that faith.

Irreplaceable Intercession

In recent years, the perseverance of the saints has been increasingly referred to simply as "eternal security." While the term itself is not wrong, it lacks specificity and clarity about the details of the doctrine. Calling it eternal security makes it sound like the believer's eternal life is external and automatic. It plays into false mentality of "once saved, always saved"—the idea that praying a prayer, walking an aisle, or some other simple claim of faith is all it takes to secure salvation. That perspective woefully overlooks the vital intercessory work of Christ that secures our perseverance in the faith.

In John 17, we see our Lord, the Great High Priest, interceding on behalf of His people. This is an inside look into how Jesus prays—the same way He prayed for Peter. He says: "I am no longer in the world; and yet they themselves are in the world, and I come to You. Holy Father, keep them in Your name" (v. 11). This is how Jesus prays for all whom the Father gives Him throughout all redemptive history. He asks that they be kept in the Father's name. He pleads for the Father to protect their faith.

> I do not ask You to take them out of the world, but to keep them from the evil one. They are not of the world, even as I am not of the world. Sanctify them in the truth; Your word is truth. As You sent Me into the world, I also have sent them into the world. For their sakes I sanctify Myself, that they themselves also may be sanctified in truth. I do not ask on behalf of these alone, but for those also who believe in Me through their word; that they may all be one; even as You, Father, are in Me and I in You, that they also may be in Us, so that the world may believe that You sent Me. The glory which You have given Me I have given to them, that they may be one, just as We are one; I in them and You in Me, that they may be perfected in unity, so that the world may know that You sent Me, and loved them, even as You have loved Me. Father, I desire that they also, whom You have given Me, be with Me where I am, so that they may see My glory which You have given Me. (vv. 15–24)

That is the constant prayer of our Lord that those who are His would be kept from the power of the evil one, sanctified by the Word of God, and ultimately brought to share in His eternal holiness and glory. He essentially says, "Father, bring those You have given Me to glory." He desires that the redeemed would be brought to glory, that they would persevere to the end. This is the prayer in view in Hebrews 7:25: "Therefore He is able also to save forever those who draw near to God through Him, since He always lives to make intercession for them."

The believer's perseverance is secured by the nonstop intercessory work of the Lord. Christ's work guarantees our salvation all the way to glorification.

From regeneration to glory, He sustains and protects the faith of His people. Jeremiah 32:40 says, "I will make an everlasting covenant with them that I will not turn away from them, to do them good; and I will put the fear of Me in their hearts so that they will not turn away from Me." Salvation is an everlasting covenant. There are no dropouts; no one falls through the cracks.

Again, the doctrine of perseverance does not say believers are secure no matter what they do—it says they will persevere. It says they will persevere because the life that is in them is eternal life. It is the life of God in the soul of man, and it is sustained in every believer by the intercessory work of Christ and the Spirit according to the purpose of God.

An Abiding Hope

That had to be good news to the original recipients of this letter. Peter was writing to scattered believers in Asia Minor who were facing horrible persecution. These believers feared for their lives. More than that, they feared that their faith would fail when put to the test. They rightly did not trust in their own strength.

From the outset of his letter, Peter spoke directly to those fears. They did not need to fear threats, danger, persecution, suffering, or even death. They did not need to be intimidated or troubled by the worst that could befall them, because their eternal life would never fail. Instead of giving them doses of sympathy and commiseration, Peter pointed them to their absolute safety in Christ. They might lose all earthly possessions—they might even lose their lives—but they would never lose their salvation. Their heavenly inheritance was fixed and guaranteed, and they were being kept secure until its fulfillment. Their faith would survive anything because it is part of the eternal life God had granted them.

Consider that our eternal life includes a hope that cannot fail. Peter says that we have been "born again to a living hope through the resurrection of Jesus Christ from the dead" (1 Peter 1:3). Jesus told His disciples, "Because I live, you will live also" (John 14:19). Christ grants to us that very life that He possesses, which death cannot destroy, and so we have a living hope. Hebrews 6:19 says, "This hope we have as an anchor of the soul, a hope both sure and steadfast." Our hope cannot die because our hope is attached to our life, which is eternal. It is alive. That is the heart of the doctrine of the perseverance of the saints. We persevere because we have a life that cannot die, and that life has a promised hope that will be fulfilled.

To further bolster our hope, Peter directs our attention to

"an inheritance which is imperishable and undefiled and will not fade away, reserved in heaven for you" (1 Peter 1:4). This inheritance is guaranteed as surely as Jesus Christ rose from the dead and purchased eternal life for us. We have an inheritance already waiting for us that is "imperishable"—*aphthartos* in the Greek—which means that it's not liable to pass away, that it is eternal, indestructible, and safe with God. Not only that, but Peter also says it is "undefiled" (*amiantos*)—that is, it's unstained, and it's not subject to defect or failure. It cannot be polluted, tarnished, or touched with anything that is evil. It's also "unfading" (*amarantos*), which is to say it cannot decay or lose its supernatural beauty.

Peter is effectively echoing the words of the Apostle Paul in Colossians 3:1–2: "Therefore if you have been raised up with Christ, keep seeking the things above, where Christ is, seated at the right hand of God. Set your mind on the things above, not on the things that are on earth." Everything in this life is subject to the curse. It's prone to corruption, decay, and fading. On the other hand, our eternal inheritance is incorruptible, undefiled, and unfading. It will never be stolen, defaced, defiled, or corroded. We persevere in this eternal life because its very essence holds a living hope for our heavenly home and the life to come, which cannot change.

A Steadfast Faith

Peter highlights a second facet of the believer's eternal life—our living faith. He says that we are "protected by the power of God through faith for a salvation ready to be revealed in the last time" (1 Peter 1:5). Our hope lives because saving faith cannot fail. We will believe all the way into eternal glory. Never do we cease to believe.

And how is this undying faith sustained? Ephesians 2:8 says, "For by grace you have been saved through faith; and that not of yourselves, it is the gift of God." This faith is not natural or human but rather a supernatural ability to believe the truth concerning God and the gospel throughout the entirety of our lives. It is not apart from our own will, but by divine power it activates our will, and we remain steadfast—not passive, but active in the persevering.

The "salvation ready to be revealed in the last time" is a look ahead to our final and ultimate deliverance from sin. It's the last aspect in the threefold glories of our salvation. As believers, we have been justified and saved from sin's penalty. We are presently being sanctified and saved from sin's power in our lives. And in the future, we will be glorified and saved from sin's presence altogether. Our faith in Christ guarantees it.

An Enduring Power

Not only do we persevere in this eternal life with a living hope and a living faith, but we also do so with a living power. Peter writes, "In this you greatly rejoice, even though now for a little while, if necessary, you have been distressed by various trials, so that the proof of your faith, being more precious than gold which is perishable, even though tested by fire, may be found to result in praise and glory and honor at the revelation of Jesus Christ" (1 Peter 1:6–7). There is divine power operative in our lives that sustains us through even the most severe trials of this life.

This was an important reminder for Peter's original audience, and it continues to be a source of encouragement to us to this day. He emphasizes the temporary nature of our earthly troubles: "Even though now *for a little while*, if necessary, you have been distressed by various trials" (v. 6, emphasis added). And these fleeting trials cannot compare to the "praise and glory and honor" believers will receive "at the revelation of Jesus Christ" (v. 7). Paul makes the same point in 2 Corinthians 4:17: "For momentary, light affliction is producing for us an eternal weight of glory far beyond all comparison." Nothing this world can throw at us can compare to the blessings God will bestow on those who have been given persevering faith.

In the midst of trials, many people struggle with assurance of their salvation. They ask: "Am I really saved? Have I really been forgiven? Am I really on the way to heaven?" Young people sometimes say, "I've invited Christ to be my Lord and asked God to save me many times, but I worry that I may not be a true believer." They wonder why they're being tested and struggle to find assurance.

However, it's in the midst of trials that our assurance is most strengthened. When we come through situations that could have crushed us and our faith endures, it becomes more evident that our faith is *real*. Life is full of perplexing and heartbreaking circumstances—the illnesses of people we love, tragic accidents, and shattered relationships. In all of these, our faith is tested. As those tests accumulate and we come out of them with our faith still intact despite the assaults, we have that wonderful realization, "more precious than gold" (1 Peter 1:7), that our faith is truly a gift from God that cannot fail.

False faith, on the other hand, doesn't last. Consider the parable of the soils (Matt. 13:3–9, 18–23), where the soil receives the seed, but when tribulation and trouble come, they choke the seed and it dies without ever having fruit (vv. 20–21). That is a false faith. Or the love of riches and the cares of the world can choke that seed (v. 22). The people who lose their faith in a trial—the ones who shake their fist at God and walk away—are the rocky and thorny soils. The seed never truly took root in their hearts. They never had real faith to begin with.

But real faith emerges from trials stronger than it was before. The greatest thing that the Lord can give a believer is a hard trial that proves the validity of his saving faith. There is distress for a season and it is necessary, because it perfects our faith. Isn't that what James says? "Consider it all joy, my brethren, when you encounter various trials, knowing that the testing of your faith produces endurance. And let endurance have its perfect result, so that you may be perfect and complete, lacking in nothing" (James 1:2–4). Trials come like fire to burn off the dross, and that is the point. What's left is the power to overcome and a stronger faith. We persevere because we have eternal life, and that eternal life consists of a living hope, a living faith, and a living power that can never die.

A Lasting Love

Our eternal life also includes a love that never fails. If you want to define Christianity in the simplest terms possible, it is this: Christians love Christ. First Peter 1:8 says, "And though you have not seen Him, you love Him." We are defined by that love. "If anyone does not love the Lord, he is to be accursed" (1 Cor. 16:22). Christians are those who love God in return for the love He has poured out on us. "We love, because He first loved us" (1 John 4:19). We have an undying love for Christ.

Our love for Christ is not merely affection or emotion. It's a desire to obey Him—to serve, sacrifice, and glorify the Lord. Jesus said, "He who has My commandments and keeps them is the one who loves Me" (John 14:21). Although we have not seen Christ, we devote our lives to worship Him and to do the work of His kingdom.

In another familiar passage regarding the perseverance of the saints, the Apostle Paul described the lasting, unwavering love between God and His people.

Who will separate us from the love of Christ? Will tribulation, or distress, or persecution, or famine, or nakedness, or peril, or sword? . . . But in all these things we overwhelmingly conquer through Him who loved us. For I am convinced that neither death, nor life, nor angels, nor principalities, nor things present, nor things to come, nor powers, nor height, nor depth, nor any other created thing, will be able to separate us from the love of God, which is in Christ Jesus our Lord. (Rom. 8:35, 37–39)

Our eternal life is marked by a lasting, singular love for our Savior—a love that's manifest in our desire to serve Him and His people.

A Permanent Joy

The perseverance of the saints is rooted in our eternal life in Christ, which includes a living hope, a living faith, a living power, a living love, and a living joy. Peter said, "Though you do not see Him now, but believe in Him, you greatly rejoice with joy inexpressible and full of glory" (1 Peter 1:8). That joy is manifest in a believer because it is an element of eternal life. David wrote, "You have put gladness in my heart" (Ps. 4:7) and "Let the righteous be glad; let them exult before God; yes, let them rejoice with gladness" (Ps. 68:3).

No matter what is happening in our lives—no matter how hard the persecution is, no matter how difficult the trials are or how tough the suffering is—God's people have a deep, unassailable joy in the anticipation of future glory. We can rejoice in every situation because we rest in the loving provision and care of our Father, and our eyes are fixed on our future with Him. In fact, we look beyond painful and disappointing circumstances to the unfolding redemptive plan of God and find joy and comfort in the progress of His kingdom. Jesus told His disciples in the upper room, "These things I have spoken to you so that My joy may be in you, and that your joy may be made full" (John 15:11). Our joy is impervious to the vicissitudes of *this life* because our joy has nothing to do with this life; it flows out of our *eternal life*.

We see these realities present in our lives, don't we? Hope, faith, love, power, and joy—the believer experiences these as components of eternal life in Christ. They are the ever-present evidence of our true faith, and it is in the reality of these heavenly gifts that we persevere.

An Eternal Outcome

In the end, Peter writes, we persevere as we look forward to our glorification. He describes this glorification as "obtaining as the outcome of your faith the salvation of your souls" (1 Peter 1:9). Our final glorification is the ultimate element of the new life we possess in Christ. It is the culmination and fulfillment of our hope, faith, love, power, and joy. Looking ahead to eternity with God, we persevere and cling to the promise in the words of the Apostle Paul: "He who began a good work in you will perfect it until the day of Christ Jesus" (Phil. 1:6). On that day, Christ will complete the work He has begun in us.

Until then, He bids us to remain. Speaking in the upper room, after Judas had been revealed and dismissed, Jesus spoke to His disciples. He said: "I am the true vine, and My Father is the vinedresser. Every branch in Me that does not bear fruit, He takes away; and every branch that bears fruit, He prunes it so that it may bear more fruit. You are already clean because of the word which I have spoken to you" (John 15:1–3). He was talking about Judas—the prototypical fruitless branch that is cut off. Christ said, "If anyone does not abide in Me, he is thrown away as a branch and dries up; and they gather them, and cast them into the fire and they are burned" (v. 6). Such are the consequences for those with false faith, who, like Judas, cannot persevere.

Our Lord told His eleven remaining disciples, "Abide in Me" (v. 4). Christianity has taken that word "abide" and turned it into something mystical. What was Jesus really saying to them? He was urging them to remain faithful to their calling, to not do what Judas did, to demonstrate by perseverance that their faith was the real thing, given by the Lord. And they did, as all true believers will do too.

All that God does to secure our persevering faith does not preclude obedience to His commands by believers. We are kept by the power of God, through faith in hope, love, peace, and joy—but not apart from our willing devotion to remain faithful by pursuing all the means of grace.

NOTES

Chapter One

1 Richard Sibbes, *Commentary on 2 Corinthians Chapter 1*, in *Works of Richard Sibbes*, ed. Alexander B. Grosart (Edinburgh, Scotland: Banner of Truth, 1981), 3:208.

2 Sibbes, *Commentary on 2 Corinthians Chapter 1*, in *Works*, 3:210–11.

3 *The Works of John Owen*, ed. William H. Goold (Edinburgh, Scotland: Banner of Truth, 1967), 6:14.

4 Wayne W. Dyer, *Your Erroneous Zones* (New York: Funk & Wagnalls, 1976), 90–91.

5 Colin G. Kruse, *The Second Epistle of Paul to the Corinthians*, The Tyndale New Testament Commentaries (Grand Rapids, Mich.: Eerdmans, 1995), 70–71.

6 Charles Wesley, "I Want a Principle Within," 1749.

Chapter Two

1 Geza Vermes, *The Complete Dead Sea Scrolls in English*, rev. ed. (London: Penguin, 2004), 98.

2 Vermes, *Complete Dead Sea Scrolls*, 99.

3 Dietrich Bonhoeffer, *The Cost of Discipleship*, trans. R.H. Fuller, 2nd rev. ed. (Philadelphia: Westminster, 1960), 163.

4 R.C.H. Lenski, *The Interpretation of St. Matthew's Gospel* (Minneapolis: Augsburg, 1964), 247.

5 Bonhoeffer, *The Cost of Discipleship*, 166.

6 For a fuller discussion of God's comprehensive love for mankind, see chapter 5 of my book *None Other: Discovering the God of the Bible* (Orlando, Fla.: Reformation Trust, 2017).

Chapter Four

1   John Calvin, *Calvin's New Testament Commentaries*, trans. A.W. Morrison (Grand Rapids, Mich.: Eerdmans, 1972), 1:207.

2   A.W. Tozer, *The Knowledge of the Holy* (New York: Harper & Row, 1961), 42.

3   D. Martyn Lloyd-Jones, *Studies in the Sermon on the Mount* (Grand Rapids, Mich.: Eerdmans, 1974), 2:67–68.

Chapter Five

1   For more on these attempts to renovate the gospel and widen the grace of God, see chapter 3 of my book *Good News: The Gospel of Jesus Christ* (Orlando, Fla.: Reformation Trust, 2018).

SCRIPTURE INDEX

ABOUT THE AUTHOR

Dr. John MacArthur is pastor-teacher of Grace Community Church in Sun Valley, Calif., president of The Master's University and Seminary, and president and featured teacher with the Grace to You media ministry.

Founded in 1969, Grace to You is the nonprofit organization responsible for developing, producing, and distributing Dr. MacArthur's books, audio resources, and the *Grace to You* radio and television programs. *Grace to You* radio airs more than fifteen hundred times daily throughout the English-speaking world, reaching major population centers with verse-by-verse exposition of Scripture. It also airs nearly a thousand times daily in Spanish, reaching twenty-three countries across Europe and Latin America. All of Dr. MacArthur's sermons are available at the ministry website (gty.org) at no charge.

Dr. MacArthur has written nearly four hundred books and study guides, including *The Gospel according to Jesus, The Gospel according to the Apostles, Ashamed of the Gospel, Twelve Ordinary Men, Truth Endures, Slave, Strange Fire, Parables, None Other, The Gospel according to Paul, Good News, The Gospel according to God*, and the MacArthur New Testament Commentary series. His titles have been translated into more than two dozen languages. *The MacArthur Study Bible*, the cornerstone resource of his ministry, is available in English, Spanish, Russian, German, French, Portuguese, Italian, Arabic, and Chinese.